POLITICAL COVID

HOW AUSTRALIA'S LEADERSHIP
PLAYED THE PANDEMIC
(and other political stories)

Andrew Laming

Connor Court Publishing Pty Ltd

Published in 2023 by Connor Court Publishing Pty Ltd.

Connor Court Publishing Pty Ltd.
PO Box 7257
Redland Bay QLD 4165
sales@connorcourt.com
www.connorcourt.com

ISBN: 9781922815354

Cover picture by Andrew Laming

Printed in Australia.

contents

published op-eds

first speech 2004

foreword

I didn't like Lammo when we first met as trainee ophthalmologists. Too intense. Talked too much. Opinionated at an age when most of us just wanted to fit in. Tall stories about clearing landmines in Afghanistan and working in the outback (which all turned out to be true).

Damn bright though, probably a genius, I thought, as he crammed and passed his Ophthalmology specialists exam whilst simultaneously opening a gym, setting up an Indigenous research project in the Northern Territory and starting a charity. Frankly hyperactive. Usually running late or not at all.

Then another career change; throwing away a 500k Ophthalmogy job to pursue a Masters of Public Admin at Harvard University and then another variety of charitable public health initiative; then finally a career in politics.

As an observer and later a good friend of Andrew's, I came to realise that he was a genuine and deeply caring person, insatiably curious and the first to jump in to help whether asked (or not). Very persistent when activated!

His impulsivity and reduced verbal filter were a gift and yet a curse as a politician. I suspect every Liberal Prime Minister had a Lammo management plan to bring him back onto the reservation when he went off script.

We need people like Lammo in politics to cut through the crap and bring ideas to the parliament. Yet the discipline of being "on message" and the boredom of rigid party orthodoxy will always be a challenge.

When Lammo asked me to foreword this book, he said, "just go hard", say whatever you want. From what I understand, the contents of his book will be no different.

Dr Peter Sumich
MBBS (Hons.), FRANZCO, FRCOphth.

1

a beginning of sorts

The Canberra office phone rang, and it was Scott Morrison. This was the 2018 day before he would sweep the party room and seize prime minister from a mortally wounded Malcolm Turnbull.

It was also a couple of days after I pledged my support to Peter Dutton. So the window for counteroffers had closed. I simply didn't have it in me to turncoat on a fellow Queenslander. It was a decision that would cost me big time.

My bones told me after that phone call with Morrison that he would swamp Dutton and win. His case was simply too polished, and workshopped to perfection. He would be too compelling for my colleagues south of the Tweed to resist. Add to that Morrison had no drag to his name, having turned to electoral gold each portfolio he held. As anticipated, his calls moved seismically through the Coalition offices; mopping up the remnants of Turnbull supporters and guaranteeing the next Prime Minister would not be from Queensland.

The Hobson's choice had its origins in a disturbingly early phone call to my Civic apartment at the start of that same sitting week. It was Malcolm Turnbull and not yet 6.30 am.

"If there are any moves on the leadership today Andrew, would you support me?"

Only half a step from deep sleep at that hour, I responded, "Sure Malcolm, you got it."

Like the others who were called, we had no idea it was Malcolm who would not only carry a knife but start the fight just hours later by calling for challengers.

By 10am, the brightly coloured voting ballots were disseminating across the room and having been artfully wedged that morning by the boss, I forced myself write Turnbull. The room seethed with shock more than resignation. But it wasn't our first rodeo. I whipped out my phone and photographed my ballot for good measure.

As we filtered out of party room, fellow members were grasping the reality of the narrow 45-36 Turnbull win. But I was consumed with a larger issue. I don't often text Peter Dutton but late the previous night I had offered him support in a text, should he ever make a move. I had no idea what would be visited upon the party room the following morning.

The moment I wrote Turnbull on my ballot just hours later, I had double crossed a Queensland colleague. I was unable to explain my way out of this one, so I ignored the corridor small talk and flashing media outside the Whip's office and went direct to my office. The predicament appeared impossible. Collapsing at my desk, it was Sydney MP and Turnbull numbers man Craig Laundy who rung me first.

Laundy was one of Parliament's extraordinary characters, and an incredible loss to the capital when he called it quits prematurely. Unlike the left where Parliament is pinnacle, Laundy was the exemplar the Liberal dilemma; that being a Parliamentarian is a shitty option compared to what the free market offers. He was sounding upbeat that day, but I could sense it was an effort for him.

"Lammo, I need you to come down to the Prime Minister's office PMO; I need your vote back for Malcolm and we need to talk about a portfolio." I took issue with all three. "Craig, I did vote for Malcolm; I don't want a portfolio and I won't be coming down to the PMO."

Next call was to fess up to Dutton. I scrolled through to his name to find the text and opened it. The chat box was full of text but was not the blue of a sent message. So exhausted the previous night, I had omitted to press send, meaning Dutton never got any message at all. I had dodged a bullet and with it, the derision of many of his Queensland supporters who were certain to interrogate my party room vote. That meant there was time for reprieve; the second punch on Malcolm could only be days away and Dutton was at the time the only other horse to back.

I wandered down to Dutton's hood in the Ministerial wing. His coterie was in the awkwardly named monkeypod room, where it was evident things weren't going great. His face revealed the tension of the moment, and once my support was offered in person, there was little else to talk about.

Morrison went on to win leadership that week, and just months later achieved the remarkable against Bill Shorten. When a leader pulls the rabbit and wins the unwinnable, they are conferred by MPs an unassailable authority; an aura. The heroics are recalled every time a Government rep strolls to their seat on the northern side of the Chamber. Likewise, when Turnbull nearly blew it all in 2016, that cloak of invincibility is ripped away for ever.

Returning in mid-2019 felt like the Coalition had stretched its luck like a guitar string. The Abbott/Turnbull tension was gone for the first time since 2004. Morrison was making leadership look easy. But by the end of 2019 the bloke needed a break badly. He deserved to unwind somewhere on a tropical island and come back for Australia Day.

That was the right call of course, but not the right time. The rest of the nation was either battling natural disasters or immersed in winding up the working year. Morrison's bushfire holiday detonated everything he had worked for. In just 48 hours, his aura was obliterated in a blizzard of aloha shirts.

It was the bar-b-que stopper that Abbott had been in January 2016 and again for all the wrong reasons. The Premiers did precisely the same thing, but five days later. By then the nation had switched into holiday mode, and no one was the wiser.

I would occasionally remind my colleagues of the wealth of leadership potential on the Labor side. Not just the genuine quality like Wong and Leigh, but much of Rudd's class of 2007; which had been the finest ALP recruitment in a generation.

On our side the political terrain was notably different; there was no ready replacement should we ever lose Morrison. Porter and Birmingham aside, I could not see our next leader in the current party room. Josh Frydenberg worked like a Trojan and wrote opinion articles ferociously, but I couldn't visualise him in the top job.

So we headed into 2020 with a stable but brittle Coalition configuration and plenty of time to repair the PM. He enjoyed quantum level stability, in no small part due to the team player nature of Peter Dutton. But even with two years until the likely 2022 election, I realised there were no more rabbits out of the Coalition hat. It would be all or nothing with Morrison.

My backbench role in the Morrison outfit was social policy agitation. At the zenith of Coalition fortunes three years earlier, we had Birmingham in Education, Hunt in Health and the Morrison/Porter nexus in social policy. It was the dream team. But after 2019, two of the three moved on. Morrison was now too distracted. Michaela Cash mired in mostly pointless Industrial Relations squabbles and Ruston was a shadow of Porter.

The Coalition's welfare reform agenda had stalled with Porter's shift to Attorney General. A key casualty was probably the last legislative reform I wanted to land before leaving Parliament; a drug testing trial for jobseekers who fail to meet their mutual obligations.

I pressed Ruston week after week until it became obvious, she had no intention of continuing the work of her predecessor. "Don't worry," Ruston told me in a moment of honest frustration, "we can pick all this up again after we win the next 2022 Election."

I had vacated health policy after my shadow portfolio was handed to the Nationals in 2016 and instead focussed on the early education sector. With my Parliamentary friends of Early Learning thriving,

I drove the expansion of the US Abecedarian program which was picked up by three states. With Greg Hunt, my priority was wider adoption of Medicare primary care item numbers for vulnerable children, to secure the allied health care they needed. It was hard to imagine a more important social policy area than children whose home conditions destroy their chances of succeeding at school.

Indigenous policy must be near the top of any priority list, but it was in the all-too-hard basket. My Coalition colleagues were right that there was no political dividend for the slog required. Since Rudd's 2007 national apology, the entire Indigenous sector had become obsessed with symbolism, climaxing in closures of Uluru and Wollumbin, opposing the national day and generally cancelling stuff. Constitutional recognition was demanded before we even knew what the Voice would look like.

Indigenous Australians don't need white permission for a Voice, nor our approbation. Just book a Convention Centre, the required airline flights and accommodation, and get on with it. Australians want facts on the ground, practical improvements in household income and with it, gaps automatically close. The suggestion that a Voice is ignored by MPs unless it is embedded in the Constitution is ridiculous.

Instead, we have urban air-conditioned activists immersed in the symbolism wars. Ken Wyatt identified that; artfully accommodating these viewpoints, deflecting them, and neutralising any electoral backlash on the Coalition.

The annual close the gap statements to Parliament were excruciating; each new year saw regression to the mean, as a new gap narrowed slightly and were celebrated. Related was the latter-day stampede to Indigenous identification; driven too often by pursuit of benefit or subsidy. The more Indigenous population data was skewed with new recruits from middle Australia, the more gaps appeared to be closing when they weren't.

At university in 1990, I rationalised the political spectrum in Australia as a vexed choice between two major parties; pushing social policy reform to conservatives in the Coalition; or flogging economic reason to a party of social progress. I chose the former, my Harvard mate Andrew Leigh and the inimitable Joel Fitzgibbon the latter.

Being party outsiders meant cutting our cloth to suit the purse. The Sydney Morning Herald's James Massola generously referred to my approach 'so mercurial as to be an independent.' Canberra can be a daunting and impervious wall flanked by two heaving ideologies. Both are happy to fight for trenches and never give an inch. Some in Canberra relish that battle, never averting their gaze from sworn enemies, who dutifully reciprocate.

Among them yet detached are a few who see the excess, the irrationality and how much that is good gets lost in that struggle. Outsiders identify seams of opportunity; detonating what can't be defended, then plugging the wall with something better. That is my kind of politics. We won't ever erect an entirely new wall this way, but it is a better wall that changes lives where it matters, and in time, the old wall becomes unrecognisable.

There are boundless opportunities in politics to iron out 'injustices with tiny ripples of hope and crossing each other from a million different centres of energy.' That was how Robert F Kennedy described it. While surely more ambitious in goal, his method was equally applicable today. When my 2004 first speech quoted Kennedy from his 1966 Cape Town masterpiece, an attentive John Howard leaned across from the dispatch box to his freshly promoted Parliamentary Secretary Christopher Pyne. "Sounds like he is another one of yours." The great man was on the money.

2

Covid calls

February 2020 was me sneaking out of Australia just as Covid was sneaking in.

Direct to Westminster, it was door-to-door meetings before happening upon Theresa May walking alone to Treasurer Rishi Sunak's Budget speech. She was calm and at that moment I sensed Covid was just another issues brief. Sitting behind a beaming George Brandis in the Parliamentary gallery, we enjoyed a view of the sardine can. Social distancing was yet to enter our lexicon.

In that week by chance, Covid case rates in both the UK and Australia were comparable. I calculated in my head that both nations were both around 10 cases per million adults. These two closest of allies were in the starter's hands in a race that would be measured by lives lost and currency burned. It was a coincidence that started me on a route I might otherwise never have embarked; comparative analysis of epidemic management.

The week before the London trip, I had shoe-horned in a Frydenberg electorate visit; hosting him nearby at Brisbane's impressive Howard Smith wharves. Hoping for some insight from above, it was clear the leadership had no clearer picture than me of what was about to steal two years from everyone's lives.

More concerning at the time was Josh's management of a solitary climate change interjector who found a way into the sea of suits. Just as Frydenburg was opening, the front row heckler hit his stride, demanding from the Treasurer precisely what action the Government was taking to cool the planet.

These moments are never easy, but Josh elected to freeze and simply stare at the back wall until the annoyance was gone. The stalemate was a train wreck for the event. In any other circumstance security would charge in, unleash some ju jitsu finger hold and frog march the guy out. But balmy Brisbane was far too nice a place for that. So much so, Josh had stood down his security detail who were instead sipping coffee down the street. In horror and out of options, I leapt to the stage and engaged the intruder in some rudimentary Q and A. I couldn't fathom why a future leadership contender would handle a lone interjector in such a way.

Fast forward to London weeks later and the bad coffee was wearing thin. Morrison confirmed everyone's suspicions by announcing international borders would close that coming Sunday, just 13 hours after the return leg was scheduled to land in Brisbane. I stuck with the booking, slinked through Immigration, alerted the CMO to my movements, and received the 'all clear.'

Spared international quarantine by only a few hours, first order of business was to set up my own Covid model on excel. The Commonwealth posted daily data from the states. At the same time, sentinel cases in other lead economies offered a time zero that shone a light on the actual replication rate on the ground here.

Within days it was clear data the first wave was not even close to exponential. Looking at Chinese data, it wasn't there either. But outside New Zealand, it was hard to find a comparable economy because the northern hemisphere was in the midst of its winter flu season. I knew Australia's kinder climate, lower residential densities, low levels of intergenerational accommodation and better public health conferred some innate advantage. Question was would the data bear that out.

Back in Canberra, the replication rate was uncertain, and we were reassured it was all in hand. By 28 March I had sufficient trend data to model both the peak and decline of new cases. My calculations suggested restrictions could be eased in less than a month. So I backed the analysis and told my local media. Crickets.

The day after my forecasts ran, no one had picked up the story. Next I tried my fledgling Twitter account; "This thing will be under control in 3-4 weeks," hoping someone out there would bite.

On cue, in came *The Guardian*'s Amy Remeikis, sputtering that "one MP" doesn't agree with Scott Morrison's "new normal." Labor MPs took the bait and launched their own attacks. But my numbers held, and exactly "three to four weeks later", on 26 April, Premier Palaszczuk indeed announced the first Covid relaxations.

It was already clear that Chief health officers were puppets to their masters; the Premiers. Advice remained secret, appearing to be tailored to the political needs of the day. Commonwealth advice from the Chief Medical Officer did appear on the Australian Health Protection Principal Committee (AHPCC) website, but states developed their Covid advice behind the closed doors of public health units.

Emboldened by my results, the next step was these holding public health colleagues accountable for their doomsday modelling. There was little upside to ever being less conservate than their colleagues. It generated a race to predict the most doom; including the Doherty scenarios of 25,000 deaths which were based upon completely implausible 'do-nothing' scenarios. Fancy modelling was put before the newly formed National Cabinet and adopted with little question.

The first wave had its challenges; Victoria declined Morrison's offer of Defence assistance. The *Ruby Princess* was disembarked on the advice of some never previously seen or heard NSW public health expert group. Premiers ran tedious and choreographed press conferences, flanked by concerned clinicians. For hours media obsessed over these performances, with naïve Chief health officers used as political pawns, just as the politicians were trying to sound like the public health officials.

I was sympathetic to Morrison's bind in National Cabinet. He was hostage to Premiers; too often gimped into submission where he should have held firm. The consensus of Premiers and their special interests was at times, a mile from the actual science. Thanks to bandwagon effect, no party wanted to go it alone.

Rather than performing natural experiments in various states to see what was effective, National Cabinet amounted to a copy-cat race to the bottom. Ruby Princess aside, Gladys Berejiklian was the stand-out performer. Close second was South Australia's Steven Marshall who too often didn't push his sensible agendas at National Cabinet, lest it destabilise the Prime Minister.

Covid response becomes dysfunctional

If the dubious Doherty modelling was being lapped up in Treasury, it explains the massive fiscal overreaction that followed. It was clear Treasury served up GFC-type fiscal stimulus, and it was accepted with little revision. By the time it arrived at the party room a few days later, there was zero latitude for any revisions.

The learnings from the GFC era were simple; to be timely, temporary and targeted. Rudd blew the targeted and temporary components but had Turnbull's full support in being timely.

For obvious reasons, politicians are the last people capable of targeting. That is where Treasury should have assisted but failed to. In the rush to be timely, their Covid response design was ugly from the outset. The only upside was that by being so poorly targeted, there were apart from self-funded retirees, so few 'losers' that the subject rarely came up. But as a policy purist, it was a struggle to swallow such obvious and avoidable flaws.

Clearly the bureaucrats didn't want to face any question of being 'slow to act' and to their credit, a range of policies requiring significant preparation were ready to roll from 20 March 2020. But this was no 2008 financial crisis with lifetimes of savings destroyed. The Covid pandemic was a government response to a health crisis requiring compensation for those furloughed or briefly unemployed.

Jobseeker bonuses and JobKeeper payments to business had a common challenge; how to target those genuinely affected. It was coarse in design and paid too many people, long after it was clear payments weren't required. There was no mechanism go recover unnecessary payments after the fact.

While these transfers were meant to be in place to ease the hard landing for the many anticipated to lose their jobs, the same payment went to the 800,000 currently out of work. It was simply a bonus cheque of around $8,000 over the ensuing months.

JobKeeper had similar challenges; paid to business anticipating a 30% fall in revenue, regardless of what impact that had on their employment.

This was no sustained shock. Job vacancies had recovered 78% by September 2020, but the moral hazard of JobKeeper payments made these jobs challenging to re-fill. We needed solutions to both, but the impression in the corridors was that any policy change would only concede the initial design was flawed.

JobKeeper fix

On 6 April 2020, it was obvious the flat-rate JobKeeper payment far exceeded the earnings lost for those working just a few hours a week. It was creating a 'shit storm' of moral hazard that would leave thousands at home effectively refusing to come back to work.

I put to Frydenberg that we introduce three payment tiers so that those working just a few hours get $500 per fortnight rather than $1500, $1000 for 15-30 hours, and the $1500 payment reserved for full time workers. With that money reimbursed to business, many of the low-hours employees could have been eligible for jobseeker and collected JobKeeper top-up if they showed up to work. I emailed Frydenberg, his advisors and then addressed the economic bank bench committee. Josh didn't get it, his staff didn't brief him and at the backbench phone hook-up, it was like I was speaking in a different language. My billion dollar dilemma was met with silence, before the agenda rolled on to the next comment from some other colleague upset that a pizza shop in their electorate had missed out on payments.

Back to the advisors, I re-iterated the tiered payment model, then demanded a one-on-one with Frydenberg. Josh was completely overwhelmed. Out of courtesy I suspect, he finally 'got it,' implying it had all been indecipherable to his army of economists up to that point. My idea was noted and that was it. The train had left the station, The flat rate for all workers would remain, regardless of hours they worked.

Set in stone, I switched to re-opening parts of the service sector where it was safe, with a mask and some common sense. With the Australian refractory after publishing my piece the previous week, Julie Lewis at the *Herald* took a second look, but had reservations. "I'm still not sure you've supplied enough evidence (reopening the service sector) is a safe move. Sounds like Sweden to me and I don't think (they) are heading in the right direction." It made the cut on 2 May, and the access to Fairfax readers was critical. At a billion dollars per working day, lockdowns weren't something that could run forever. We had to build pressure on Labor premiers to take their collective feet off the throat of their own economies.

My last opportunity was to have the JobKeeper amended in the Senate. I reached out to Pauline Hanson adviser James Ashby and they got it immediately and made it their policy position. But it rolled through the Upper House as it was. Five months later, Treasury implemented the tiered model I proposed, billions of dollars later than they should have.

Jobseeker supplement

The jobseeker supplement was even harder to justify. Self-funded retirees (SFRs) woke up to it overnight and they were furious. The contrast could not be more extreme; we were paying those least likely to vote Coalition an $8,000 bonus, leaving MPs explaining to their most trenchant supporters why they were not getting a cent. MPs were forced to remind SFRs they should spend down their assets to get through. Many simply couldn't liquidate assets on the spot, let alone survive in the near zero interest rate environment.

In June 2020 I proposed jobseekers continue receiving their regular allowance, with any extra supplement accumulating as a work subsidy. Centrelink already operated a half-hearted job credit arrangement, so it didn't require any new design.

The modification would see future supplements accumulating as an employment incentive, because it would be released at the same $550 a fortnight rate, but only as soon as work commenced. Better still, the employer only had to pay the top-up to the award wage, meaning the larger the accrued supplement, the more attractive jobseekers were to employers. As with other programs, substitution of subsidised for existing workers would not be permitted.

It wasn't the simplest policy, but it represented a once in a generation opportunity to address the fact that employees less productive than the minimum wage have awful employment prospects. We had time to get this transfer arrangement right and thousands could be engaged in the non-profit sector and outdoor community projects at Council level.

hunting

In this new world of Covid prohibitions, there was little appetite for a measured approach. The political risk of criticism for an inadequate response was simply too great. My view was that the precautionary approach justified going hard early, but once the science was available, we had to start being guided by it, rather than by fear or political self-preservation. State Governments as service providers didn't have a dog in the fight. It was the Commonwealth writing the cheques that did.

In a 6 April 2020 message, three weeks after I was back from the UK, I updated Greg Hunt on the Queensland situation; "Queensland is unlikely to go over 500-1000 cases in this wave; we need to allow fitness with masks, and not ban family groups from dining out together. Mass gatherings and Aged Care are the real threats", I reiterated.

State governments were at times slow to report their recovered cases. This artificially inflated total case numbers, delayed Covid peaks and allowed Premiers to overstate the crisis. I caught Victoria out, not reporting ventilated cases, and Hunt confirmed there appeared to be "reporting issues." "Their numbers are too good to be true," I told him on 6 April. Inquiries must have followed, with a huge pulse of serious cases added the next day; a notch in their reporting data is still visible today.

The Government was relieved to be landing 30 million masks and that their protective equipment supply lines were holding. But sick of waiting around for a bumbling procurement taskforce, an old mate Brendon Hempel was in Melbourne, arranging to land 250 million masks in up to seven A330 flights, packed with PPE.

"Is that 250,000 or million?" Hunt inquired. "Yes Greg; million." The private sector were simply hungrier and more agile than his department was. It also served as a harbinger for the rapid antigen (RAT) test fiasco that would smash our government in 2021. We should have given confidence to the private sector to sort-out supply issues, including approving many more RAT tests by mid-2021.

There was reluctance in Canberra to agree to any policy that put them on the hook to pay. By this point National Cabinet unity was close to non-existent, so the party ordering the RAT tests would inevitably be forced to pay for them.

hospitals in neutral

The one thing killing more people than Covid ever would was the bizarre overreaction to shut down non-emergent hospital activity. In my opinion, we panicked early that PPE supplies would run short and our ICUs would be overrun. These factors were relied upon by experts because they are almost impossible to disprove. It led to widespread and irrational shutdowns of elective surgery and outpatients. The paralysis of hospital care around the country was a handy fiscal saving for the states; a decision which killed thousands more Australians than Covid did, as it did overseas.

Australia's Bureau of Statistics didn't help. The ABS has always delayed reporting causes of death, by virtue of excluding coronial referrals which can take months to resolve. Europe simply gets on with reporting that data then adjusting it later; something the ABS piously declines to do. The cost is we don't get death data until far later in the piece, and any net increase in deaths during lockdown are only revealed months later when it was too late to do anything about it. I urged Michael Sukkar to push a little harder, but I realised even his pushing would be futile.

The verdict finally came through when no one really cared; lockdowns killed inordinately more people than Covid but the debate could never happen early enough to matter. Far from being an argument against lockdowns, it is an argument for maintaining services that prevent more deaths than Covid does. I was always resolute that a low-replication viral epidemic should not subvert other clinical care. Nor should we fear an outbreak overwhelming one or two cities or hospitals. That is easily addressed by effort (and patient) transfer.

On 7 April 2020, again to Greg Hunt, "we can't be indefinite about closures; I nailed the peak in Queensland cases two weeks ago. Public Health officials don't get the economic situation the way MPs do. Set weekly review dates for lockdowns, not irregular ones. It's all about appearing in control and not looking like Trump."

The odd reference to the US president revealed the growing frustration with imperious media appearances of Morrison and his premiers. I had been among the colleagues who demanded decisive early action, so Hunt rightly questioned why I now sought a softening of the lockdowns, messaging me with:

"I hope I haven't got this wrong, but I did think you were the strongest advocate in the Coalition for the hardest of measures."

It was a touch simplistic to assume that support for early decisive action was inconsistent with seeking early relaxation.

"I'm an advocate for best practice," I replied.

Our path out of Covid needed to be as impressive as our path in had been. It was the only way to put us in a position to win in 2022. I urged Hunt to "drive with the PM that we combine behavioural economics with public health expertise. The latter left on its own risks overshoot. We need a hot-spots but also a 'cool-spots' approach, where localised testing and surveillance offers a return to economic normality."

modelling mania

I was furious with the apocalyptic Doherty modelling and felt Morrison was pumping it for reasons I couldn't unpick. We knew the trajectory of the disease was nothing like the doomsday predictions. Despite that, States were desperate for a clean score sheet on Covid and had no incentive to lift restrictions. After all, it was the Commonwealth picking up the tab for the farrago of COVID payments; in fact, it seemed everything except hotel quarantine was left to Canberra.

Knowing Queensland cases were falling was a big plus and it was only a matter of time before the southern states followed. Yet Hunt was still standing resolute with the modelling predictions, including that Covid could infect up to 20 million Australians. He seemed captured by the notion that there would be a risk of 'swamping and overwhelming our hospital system' if states softened any part of the response.

In frustration I shot back, saying that the half-baked modelling is just "last year's flu dynamics with an updated replication rate R0 of 2.2 thrown in." As was so often the case, we politely agreed to disagree. He responded with, "The modelling represented the unconstrained future we could have faced but have avoided." I replied "hospitals should remain alert but get on with business. To overrun EDs and ICUs from here, would require a completely different virus."

The Australian newspaper had an appetite for any view contrary to the status quo, and on 9 April published my piece "Time to run trials to find the path back to normal life."

I sent Greg Hunt my prepublication draft and received an unanticipated reply. "This will be a destructive piece ... the opening is frankly contemptuous." I responded that I felt the same about the modelling provided to National Cabinet.

I had to jump the gun with *The Australian*, since every day mattered. My modelling outcomes would not be indisputable until 20 April; effectively two latency periods or ten days following the Easter break where Premier Palaszczuk had announced the same relaxations I had predicted and called for back in late March. There was not even a blip in new cases, and from it was inevitable that save for a new outbreak flying in, that point active cases in Queensland would peak at six per million; which is not bad for a state with a population of five million.

As we turned the corner in April, we simply needed hygiene, distancing and sensible precautions. There simply was no case for draining economic reserves, massive fiscal stimulus or shutting down hospitals. Plenty shared that view, but none were inside the National Cabinet tent.

So it was a relief that around mid-April, Greg Hunt was softening. I brought to his attention that "This is the first ever fall in hospitalisations and ICU cases since this thing started." "Yesterday was" he responded. My predictions were now materialising, which Greg was kind enough to acknowledge. We had a decade long track record of collaboration, and as one of the few evidence-driven representatives, I couldn't afford to compromise the relationship.

On 13 April I pushed for the known economic costs of shutdown to be broken up by sector, calculated in collaboration with the private sector and reported. Only a sector-by-sector cost-benefit analysis would reveal what restrictions should stay and which were costing a fortune for little or no benefit. Treasury appeared to have little interest in the exercise, and the Treasurer's office didn't want uncomfortable answers to sensible questions.

"Beauty therapy may sound trivial to us," I told colleagues to their mirth, "but it puts food on thousands of people's plates – and they all wear personal protective equipment (PPE) already!" The approach appeared to be shutting down livelihoods, then seeking approbation for the $1500 a fortnight we offered with the other hand.

schools

The next policy atrocity was school closures; driven primarily by teacher union campaigns on Premiers fearing a single case in a school.

At home in Queensland, schools were shutting down without any public health evidence in the debate. To be honest it was happening in defiance of the evidence that showed children were far less likely to get infected, be far less serious, and if it did happen, catch it at home not school. But the lure for teachers to be at home was irresistible, and it was an effective Union membership drive as well.

Iceland led the way here. Kari Stefansson, founder of deCODE genetics spent nine months shadowing the virus by screening around half of the nation's 370,000 residents. There was not a single case of a child with severe symptoms; children recovered after five days and three quarters of these were mild.

Students were pushed away from school drop-off zones and working parents instructed that they 'weren't essential.' I called-out one principal just inside Bert Van Manen's electorate for conducting a stand-up sit-down exercise with students to expose publicly who didn't have essential working parents or not. Van Manen sought my apology for the call. It wasn't forthcoming.

I called for parents unable to leave their children at school to call the Police. Nine took the bait, and the following morning I would be pitted against a local State Labor MP to debate the issue. Labor rightly feared the carnage that would ensue on breakfast TV, electing to perform a switcheroo at the last minute and insert Education Minister Grace into the debate instead.

On the backfoot, I prepped Karl Stefanovic that I had just one question I wanted to ask Grace without prompting. He agreed.

I asked the Minister on air, "Can you tell me with your Covid school closures, what proportion of the Queensland school population are working parent families and how many are vulnerable? Both answers lay within the Minister's own Early Learning Strategy and ABS data, but Grace had neither figure at hand. Exposed was a Labor Minister with no idea what she was doing, who should be at school or even what an essential worker was. Grace's staff never posted the trainwreck interview. Tiktok did.

It is hard to see how preventing parents from dropping their children at school prevented a single case of any disease, but it fed a germophobic hysteria around schools that teachers accepted, despite the absence of clinical evidence to support it.

State governments claimed their vulnerable children were welcome at school, but research in my electorate using direct messaging to these families found around 95% were simply shacked up at home, because they don't self-label as vulnerable. And this confusion didn't bother the schools one bit.

pollies go awol

Credit to Canberra that the wheels kept turning, but not so in the state Parliament. Even with no community spread, the Queensland Parliamentary Speaker enforced an electorate office shut down, even though constituent contact was through the obligatory glass security screens. The reasoning was that New Zealand had done it.

Implementing a 'work from home' model was reasonable, but using it as pretext to shut down government services was not.

The Queensland Parliamentary Clerk cited 'cases' where constituents attended offices who should have been in self-isolation. It sounded like complete hearsay. On those grounds, the entire nation would be paralysed. It was the most egregious example of double standard imaginable; that elected officials making the bizarre shutdown decisions were themselves packing up and going home. Shadow Attorney General Jarrod Bleijie was copied in.

out goes the money

In Canberra, the unedited economic solutions were being trucked in from Treasury. Given the so-called urgency, policies were slipped through with minimal party room oversight and usually in retrospect. As early as 20 March 2020, I flagged with Morrison that "lending beats spending." I couldn't see why we couldn't offer lines of interest-free credit rather than empty the coffers. Known to Australians as HECS, higher education contribution scheme offered income contingent lending and was Australia's policy gift to the world. The existing mechanism was ideal to be expanded to non-welfare reliant families and to business. No response.

On 29 March 2020, I took the case up again. We were "dropping our dacks" as I described it, for what I could now see would be a fairly short first wave. "Before we spend, consider lend," I urged Morrison. Income contingent lending was the perfect tool for a crisis of uncertain duration. We could always forgive loans down the track if the need arose.

We know people treat lump-sum transfers differently to loans. The former tend towards jetski and flat screen purchases, in a way that the latter rarely does. There was every chance that over the full financial year, many businesses would turn things around and be able to pay back these advances by tax time.

This existing HECS mechanism deserved a chance because if

shutdowns were a short shock, much of the population would be unscathed. Families simply needed short-term security that they could manage a shock, rather than a pulse of fiscal stimulus to inject into the economy as we needed in 2008. It should have been about smoothing income over the short months of shutdown and ensuring obligations could be met.

Throughout the period, Ministers were under Frydenberg's spell, who in turn appeared supplicant to Treasury. They were treating a self-induced shock created by shutdowns the same way we treated a genuine financial crisis a decade earlier. There was every chance pandemics would become a regular occurrence, but the term 'once in a century' prevailed. This was the moment to test mechanisms that sufficiently opened purse strings without inflicting more economic damage than absolutely necessary. Frustratingly, it was a debate that no one in the leadership appeared willing to entertain. The full impact of the Covid fiscal overreach only revealed itself in 2022, when the inevitable inflationary pressures materialised.

dan's disaster

The darkest moment in Covid was Victorian Premier Dan Andrew's July 2020 suspension of international arrivals into Tullamarine. It precipitated a chorus of caps by each of the other States in response, none of whom wanted to risk sharing the load with Victoria. Other States should have supported Andrews in his moment of incompetence, by agreeing to share the load of repatriating Victorians. But they abandoned Victoria instead; in turn vacating the national interest. The Covid fiasco was now spinning out of control, with each state in it for themselves, and Morrison attempting to retain a veneer of control. Polling showed voters were patting the culprits on the back and it was reasonable for Morrison to cosy up and receive the same treatment.

Premiers ambushed Morrison on 6 July 2020. With Dan Andrews closing Tullamarine on political grounds, the remaining States claimed they didn't have the capacity between them to pick up the slack for Dan. Queensland at that time was using just 15 of their 2000 hotels for quarantine.

With much of the health population outside emergency care furloughed due to the shutting down non-emergent work, there were plenty of staff on hand to staff quarantine, but there was simply no political will to do so. States claimed a lack of trained staff, but half the workforce was sitting at home on JobKeeper, and there was never any intention to initiate any training if that excuse was true.

It was now clear that any single Covid case was a political disaster for Premier responsible. Repatriation fell to inhumane levels and flight costs exploded. Arriving craft were mostly empty, with stranded overseas Australians balloting for limited flights, only to have them cancelled the day prior. Many were homeless then forced into business class, only to then be hotel quarantined and fed mouldy salads. It amounted to cruel and appalling treatment, but the remarkable thing was that the rest of Australia showed little if any sympathy.

Though blame was endlessly shifted, the Commonwealth was party to abandoning citizens overseas in a way no other nation ever did. Howard Springs was brought online far too late, with Queensland Premier Palaszczuk forced into building the catastrophic quarantine facility at Wellcamp. It would ultimately serve just a few hundred arrivals, with Aspen medical charging the taxpayer around a million dollars per family. Topping it off, the Commonwealth funded its own $400 million quarantine white elephant at Pinkenba, next to Brisbane Airport. Currently, there is 'no use' for it according to Mayor Adrian Schrinner.

Queensland election loss

In late October 2020, Palaszczuk was the latest in the conga line of Covid-obsessed premiers to soft-pedal to victory. She had successfully convinced punters that cocooning the state was the right thing to do.

Ironically it was Canberra's flood of payments that did the trick.

Jobseekers were year on year around $8,000 better off thanks to the pandemic and facing not an extra cent of household expense. In addition, the $10 billion of JobKeeper payments into Queensland was boosting business bottom lines; many of which had never had it so good.

I felt for the larger southern capitals which were more densely populated and more multicultural. Their Covid challenge was more complicated, whereas Queensland used just 1% of its hotel room stock to quarantine and skated through the crisis.

Queensland had a number of small outbreaks, including a shopping trip duo who transferred via Sydney, concealing they had actually spent the weekend in Melbourne. Queensland should have accessed traveller manifests from the two major domestic airlines to prevent this, but never saw the need until it was too late.

getting them home

On 4 September, I urged the PM not to allow States to "set and forget those July inbound arrival caps." He agreed. On 6 September, I outlined the model to ensure that occurred in the Sydney Morning Herald with "Australia, you're ready for take-off."

By 13 September, I urged Education Minister Dan Tehan to push harder, but it was all being sheeted back to Premiers who were clearly in control of the inbound travel boondoggle. Strangling inbound caps saved them a fortune, and wiping out International education really wasn't their problem.

The following day I was back to Chris Daffy in Morrison's office. "Let's get Aussies home" using the charter model and re-opening Howard Springs. "Write the NT a check," I challenged. "We have to get around the blockages and States cannot refuse to quarantine an interstate transfer once they are in-country." I wanted Howard Springs to be the trojan horse, and I knew the NT Government was reasonable enough to do a deal. No response.

Lunchtime I tried again, knowing from Darwin that there had

been no offer forthcoming from Canberra at that point. "Are talks with NT proceeding mate? Howard Springs is mostly empty," I half-taunted Daffy. He responded it was a 'standing item' and that National Cabinet was meeting the following day.

There was simply no apparent connection between what Morrison was telling me and outcomes on the ground for stranded Australians. Then out of the blue I remembered a 2018 trip to Katherine, Northern Territory. I had been seconded temporarily to Chair a defence subcommittee, looking into the health impacts of PFAS contamination; a fire-fighting chemical which has leached into water tables around most of our major airports. It is a particular issue at air force bases, so a rag-tag band of MPs hit the road.

As each politician booked their own travel arrangements, they and the support staff had no choice but to drive from Darwin to Katherine because there were no commercial flights.

That changed in Katherine Show week, when the NT government suddenly negotiated commercial Darwin to Katherine flights to restart. Just in time for me to book, and completely unaware no one else was any the wiser, I ended up on the first flight, with just three others; including Chief Minister Michael Gunner.

Hardly a household face in Queensland, his advisor tapped me after the pre-flight safety talk; "Hey just to let you know, it's the Chief Minister sitting behind you." From that, I struck up a decent yarn with Gunner and it was about to pay dividends two years later, when in desperation I reached out to his office on 15 September 2020

"Why can't we use Howard Springs to repatriate Australians," I asked Gunner's office.

The response floored me. "There are around a thousand Pacific Islander workers quarantining there, so it's not exactly empty. I guess there would be room for an additional two thousand or so."

"Has anyone asked to use Howard Springs?" The answer was no.

That afternoon I went direct to Tehan and the Prime Minister's office again. We didn't need to destroy the international education sector in 2021 if we had the wherewithal to start quarantining them now. But because we were doing such an awful job with our own stranded citizens, parts of the leadership may have been nervous about the atmospherics of fast-tracking in planeloads of Asian students. Apparently only white movie stars qualified for that treatment. There was ample safe capacity in Darwin, which I imagined could ease pressure on hotel quarantine limits.

The PM gave the impression the 30,000 marooned overseas would fall as fast as the weekly repatriation totals, but this didn't account for thousands more citizens living overseas who were grabbing their Australian passport of convenience as the pandemic dragged on. The longer Covid lingered, the better Australia looked. With little warning, the repatriation queues were filled with happily overseas-domiciled citizens with ample family support in their home countries deciding the grass was greener in Australia. DFAT had no mechanism to manage the triage process, allowing applicants to fill in their own applications, without any objective questioning of the content.

Truth was, none of the Premiers wanted a solution and so Morrison had little incentive to corrode further capital by forcing them to. But no honest assessment is complete unless we note that a Commonwealth quarantine arrangement through Darwin was simply a matter of paying to make it happen. Even Border Force was in on the stalling caper, saying their AUSMAT staff were stretched, which in turn let States off the hook, by relying on the same excuse. This 'lack of staff' smokescreen was impervious to resolution.

On 23 September I pressed Gunner's office again, asking what additional help would land the deal. They were cagey, and for good reason. The first plane load of students landed into Darwin the following day and were bound for Howard Springs. Finally.

On 3 November, I could see the thousands landing were simply replaced on the never-shortening waitlist by thousands more overseas Australians coming out of the woodwork.

"Borders will be open by Christmas 2020," Morrison shot back at me. "We're getting 5,500 home per week." He thought the end was in sight. He was drinking the Kool-Aid.

mandates

The millions of Covid tests translated to massive corporate pathology profits. The nation didn't really negotiate any volume discounts, so you can understand pathologists were happy to ride the wave as long as it lasted. But is gets worse than that.

There were alternative tests called rapid antibody and rapid antigen testing RAT which came in at a fraction of the price. The gold-plated PCR was the appropriate test in the pre-vaccine era when missing a single case risked community spread.

However once at-risk Australians had been vaccine-seroconverted and the economy opened, higher Covid prevalence was inevitable, and we couldn't afford to spend millions on PCR tests that were expensive and slow. At this point, it was more important to identify Covid rapidly with home-based tests, even if the results weren't always 100%.

Rapid antigen tests (RATs) were suddenly needed as we relaxed lockdowns and the delta and omicron waves peaked. But Australia was again caught out; reinforcing the Labor position that worse than not holding the hose, Scott Morrison had forgotten to turn on the tap. It was more complicated than that, but the signs were ominous; an unusual trickle of RAT scientists into Canberra became a flow.

At the time, no one gave a RATs, because some Chinese-manufactured tests had been pulled by the FDA from the market, giving the entire category a bad wrap. But unperturbed, the quality providers persisted, and couldn't understand why the resistance was so great.

Ophthalmologist mate and polymath Peter Sumich called me from Sydney to raise the RAT issue. I wasn't convinced that 70% accuracy was the way forward, but he was persistent about the cost-benefit, so I agreed to expend a bit more political capital to confront my colleagues again.

As usual, Australia was an outlier, and the age-old defensive play was to say 'decision x which we refuse to change is part of the reason why Australia has fared so well. So I asked how the UK could distribute around 20 million RATs if we couldn't. It was Sumich who was prepared to share the evidence I couldn't easily obtain from the health establishment.

In short, the hammering RATs copped may have been due to those invested in PCR having undue influence on approvals committees. If there were any pathology representatives in this cascade of approvals, I needed to rule out any of them having a potential financial conflict. Whatever the reasons, it seemed odd that all available cost-effective technology was not on the table. By holding out, we simply undermined private sector confidence, and the orders were never placed. This may not have cost lived, but it infuriated those desperate to get back to work, and again, placed the crosshairs on the one person ultimately in charge. It was the vaccine delays all over again.

Both vaccines and RATs were firmly Commonwealth responsibilities to approve. The private sector simply needed clear signals. RATs weren't a deal-breaker in Covid management, but at a psychological level, it re-activated the nightmares of the vaccine delays to the states. I knew Palaszczuk played Morrison in this respect, but the loser in these disputes is whoever goes next to the polls. Morrison's opponents had another free swing, with the inevitable result that the Coalition was not fit to call a 2021 federal election. Just when everyone should have been winding down, a new battle was winding up; vaccine mandates.

Covid passports

Mid-2021 had seen a frisson of opposition to so-called Covid passports. It was an inflammatory term for what was effectively a worldwide system facilitating opt-in vaccine status verification. In short, it meant getting through international airports faster and a better hope of getting home should you be caught in an outbreak overseas.

On 6 August 2021, this debate morphed into workplace vaccine mandates, with food manufacturer SPC setting a 15 September staff vaccine deadline. Their case for mandating was unconvincing; it was the 'right thing to do' to 'minimise the risk to the people we care about.'

I could see this was the thin edge of the wedge and as a medical specialist was furious that we might use the pandemic to manipulate workplace culture, by threatening to sack anyone not getting the jab.

Morrison had already copped it from me earlier that same week. On 3 August I told him that "every frontline health worker needed vaccination and confirmed seroconversion" so we knew the vaccination has worked. But "there is no need to mandate vaccines beyond where the evidence supported it, because the unvaccinated can usually be deployed to safer parts of any business."

Being passionately pro-vaccine but anti-mandate, my time working in Lismore, Darwin and Hobart hospitals in the 1990s taught me mandates do about as much harm as good. For everyone roused from apathy to pull up their sleeve, another fights you on principle that wouldn't have without the mandate.

My reading was the science supported Covid vaccine mandates in all the places the flu vaccine stacked up; the health, hospital and aged care frontline, along with the NDIS and welfare sector; where chronic health issues existed. What we ended up with of course was a farrago of mandates, sackings and exemptions outside those sectors above, including terminating the person mowing the lawn for NDIS clients, or doing work-from-home travel bookings for an airline.

From experience, around 5% of the community was anti-vaccine so we could get to the magic 90% double vaccination level in good time without starting a jihad. Labor states were itching to mandate vaccines and the last thing we needed was virtue-signalling corporates following the lead.

My father Bruce said a lot of great stuff, but it seems unfair to have him remembered by the one or two pearlers recounted here. Bruce never really got religion and it's something I inherited. As a child he would say "the only reason Christianity prevailed was the Romans kept feeding them to lions." His point of course, was to avoid brutalising opponents more than we absolutely have to.

Sov-cits and libertarian extremists feed on that notoriety. They gain sympathy and support by feeding off our reaction to them. There is a propensity in the medical profession to denigrate anti-vaxxers, but I argue that achieves little. Science provides data; lawmakers the rules and we don't need crusaders. Covid muddied that separation, to the nation's detriment.

My early August workplace mandate alert to Morrison was duly ignored. But three weeks later on 28 August, he gave a nod to workplace vaccine mandates on radio, so I became more strident.

"I am bitterly disappointed with you unleashing business to make arbitrary calls … on vaccination status. This is a matter for public health orders." I reminded him the evidence for mandates was limited to health, child and aged care and the vulnerable.

Two minutes later, the Morrison fatwa was brutal: "It's a property law issue." His free market approach to health would allow each barista to set their own vaccine requirements on staff and customers. It would be months too late to save Morrison, but a small number of brave MPs and Senators would eventually flip him back.

I was managing the vaccine side-effect stories and ensuring they were registered with the TGA to be fully investigated.

But the media horror stories of fit people dropping dead rarely stacked up. I reminded outspoken Senator Gerard Rennick he could always send me his anecdotes for verification. I would also fight for deserving exemption cases where a local clinician refused. I never heard from the Senator after that.

There are a million reasons why people may be hesitant about vaccines. Sure they were not being held down and injected, but being frog-marched out of a desk job for refusing to be vaccinated was no less odious. Thankfully one of the Fair Work Commissioners took a similar view in their *Sapphire vs Kimber* decision. I knew Fair Work was watching, but that didn't help State public servants.

Queensland Health and Police workers would also take their case to the Supreme Court, but I wasn't optimistic. I urged those affected to buy as much time as they could in the hope the omicron variant come and go again within weeks. That is precisely what happened, but thousands of workers were needlessly suspended, and in the case of teachers, hundreds were bizarrely docked up to 18 weeks of pay.

Sadly, the wacky right wing anti-vaccination movement had colonized the anti-mandate campaign. Worse, they didn't understand the difference. Five percent of the community can easily fill a hall for a rally, but these anti-vaccers were essentially two typologies cancelling each other out politically. There were the green-leaning public servants horrified their hero Palaszczuk was brutalising them with a mandatory vaccine, mixed with cranky older libertarians who preference the Coalition in any case. On this basis there was utterly no upside to engaging this naïve movement. Most were captured by independent Senate candidates desperate to secure the 4% vote and electoral funding. At the point anti-vaxx and anti-mandate became inseparable, the battle was lost. Premier Anastasia Palaszczuk cleverly framed mandate opponents as being anti-vaxx. It stitched up both her Queensland LNP opposing spokespersons Ros Bates and Dr Christian Rowan. Once branded antivaxxers, the debate was over. I arranged for a number of cases to pursue delay tactics like judicial review, but the only realistic advice was to survive at work as long as possible and hope omicron subsided in early 2022.

why

National Cabinet was a Morrison creation. His reputation rode on its success. He wanted the trappings of jurisdictional unity, but even as it fell apart, he was never going to fire the first shot; something that Premiers realised and capitalised upon.

Given the complexity of policy challenges faced by Australian states, Covid presented Premiers with a welcome two-year free pass from the unrelenting pressure of underfunded service delivery. Many simply flanked themselves with a Chief Health Officer and read out the health directives handed to them. The challenge wasn't complex; transfer international arrivals to hotel rooms, swab and feed for 14 days, then hand them a $3,000 invoice. It wasn't rocket science. Even when outbreaks did occur, poorly supervised and under remunerated floor staff put the entire operation in peril. In Queensland, the Minister blamed the hotel air-conditioning.

For a decade I had worked hard to divine how Morrison's mind worked. In late 2009, he nabbed me outside the Whips office as the freshly minted Shadow spokesperson for Local Government. He had picked up whispers that I was opposed to incorporating local government into the Constitution, reminding me a little too firmly that 'a yes vote was the Coalition's formal party position.'

"It's not party policy to my knowledge Scott, and it won't be my position," I replied.

From that moment forward, I was mystified how a guy with a somewhat similar coastal outer-metro electorate could hold a policy position diametric opposed to my own. I knew there wasn't a hope in Hades my Redland City locals would vote in favour of changing anything to do with our local Council.

Then in 2012, the so-called Coalition 'yes' position on the matter was quietly dropped, with then leader Tony Abbott's infamous "if you don't understand it, don't vote for it."

Covid ends with a whimper

National Cabinet worked well to coordinate the initial crisis response but failed on the way out. The Coalition rightly felt they had borne the brunt of Covid transfers. There was a palpable reluctance to be embroiled in paying for quarantine, health cost-shifts, additional vaccine costs or rapid antigen testing.

If there was any doubt whose side the public were on through Covid, it was dispelled at the ballot box. Despite the alarming quarantine screw-ups at state level, Premiers were re-elected in a canter.

Then at the March 2022 South Australian poll, the extraordinary happened. Premier Steven Marshall delivered the best performing economy but post-Omicron, it wasn't enough. His defeat would be a dress rehearsal for the federal poll just weeks later.

By the time 2022 arrived, the Coalition had sacrificed too much of its economic standing. Waving through over $300 billion in Covid measures should have been a boon, but it sat uneasily with supporters and drained from them their appetite for an electoral fight. Debt is now indurated; increasingly something that will never be paid back. In the current climate, it's always a problem of the predecessors' making, meaning it is managed to protect the credit rating but otherwise never seriously addressed.

Deep down, Australians don't mind having their say on an election Saturday once a year. An election year was not the time to run low on vaccines, come up short with RATs or go to water on bizarre vaccine workplace mandates that extended outside healthcare, across emergency services, the travel and tourism sector, national parks, campsites and the entire public service.

After two years under the doona, Australians were ready to be unhappy again, regardless of how the money had been spent. By the end of the 46th Parliament, critics could credibly claim that the Coalition had a pass mark for Covid but little else had been achieved.

Morrison's great work in early 2020 was now a distant memory. The Covid bogeyman had receded, and voters were out of their co-

coons. Just as one changes a Hawaiian shirt, voters had little reluctance in changing their federal government.

It is a point of contention how Premiers apart from Marshall enjoyed a gentler verdict. It is a contrast which is hard to reconcile. It appears voters interpret spending hard and fast as working hard, which is translated to a favourable verdict on polling day. When the spending stops, so apparently, does the goodwill.

The Covid phenomenon stunted the policy offerings of both major parties. The 5% home-buyer deposit assistance scheme was my signature 2018 policy; adopted by Morrison for the 2019 Coalition election campaign launch. It was as much as surprise to me as anyone. Forced by its popularity to respond, Labor would later match the commitment in regional Australia, effectively guaranteeing the policy bipartisan support. The following week, the Coalition then committed to expand the program further. But policy ideas like this were few and far between.

Morrison lumbered with a broader issue around gender that fulminated with the Brittany Higgins fiasco. His panicked Parliamentary apology seemed to pre-empt the legal proceedings, while his insistence he knew nothing at the time seemed implausible.

Morrison failed every gender test he ever encountered, and the worst of them coincided with low-level policy failures that he might otherwise have negotiated unscathed. Voters only need to be mildly annoyed with a leader, to contemplate the alternative. Voters were more than mildly annoyed with him, and gender made it deeply personal for the nation's largest and most influential minority, female voters.

The palpable gender panic of the Coalition's final months in office was an inescapable fog. Morrison has clumsily invoked his family at the wrong times, so this escape route was firmly closed. Far from protecting him, his senior female Cabinet colleagues were of little assistance in the gender wars. Victorian Senator Jane hume aside, few were accomplished media performers and none enthusiastic character references. After the Christine Holgate debacle, female corporate Australia had also walked. This gave, of all people, Grace Tame the final verdict. It was a marketing train wreck in every sense of the metaphor.

published op-eds

3

Covid

Doctors should make the call on who goes to school and when
17 April 2020, *Sydney Morning Herald*

Unpicking the Covid-19 lockdown is proving far more complicated than its roll-out. While Britain and the United States are reeling from a combined 40,000 deaths so far as a result of this pandemic, Australia is paralysed over something as elementary as who should go to school, which dominated the agenda at the national cabinet meeting on Thursday.

This fact alone demonstrates the stark international differences in our Covid-19 journeys.

Sadly, much of Australia's division is party political. Premiers are tugged towards consistency by the centripetal force of the national cabinet but, back home, education unions arm-wrestle the premiers into harder lines to close down schools for all but the neediest.

The national cabinet needs to sing from one sheet. Public health has already determined that essential services can remain open. That includes schools. It is time to let the doctors do the diagnosing and teachers get on with their profession.

No teacher would determine hospital surgical priorities. So it is reasonable to ask why education unions are taking solo flights on public health. As the Prime Minister said after Thursday's meeting, teachers face more danger in the staffroom than in their classrooms. As Sting sang in his immortal tune, *Don't Stand So Close To Me*.

Australia is now reporting fewer than two new Covid-19 cases per million each day and only 2% of those are school age. There is minimal, if any, evidence that children catch or spread this disease at school.

Just three years ago, Australian schools didn't miss a beat as 1255 people died of the flu and an estimated 29,000 people were hospitalised over the season. But three years later, with just 350 Covid-19 cases in hospital, unions suddenly make their own diagnosis on school attendance.

About a third of families comprise either a single or two working parents. If their work wasn't essential, they wouldn't be getting paid.

Vulnerable children must also reconnect with school and many with special needs can't be home-schooled. Parents of these children don't wear T-shirts saying they are vulnerable, nor think they are. We are at serious risk these children simply won't show up.

Same goes for parents where appropriate care arrangements aren't available. Many home businesses can't facilitate learning at home. Often the parent that could do it is the one employed. Finally, children, who despite parents' best efforts, struggle to learn in a home environment for any unavoidable reason should be welcomed back. Only a bum of a principal would turn them away.

Much of the education union banter online has been stoking irrational teacher fears, like catching the disease from students. Teachers face more risk from other teachers and even that risk is far less than what faces the rest of the economy because teachers are isolated in classrooms for much of the working day.

More concerning are inferences that returning children returning to school is a lifestyle choice for lazy parents. In the overwhelming majority of cases, non-working parents simply trust that teachers teach better than they can. Independent Schools Queensland executive director David Robertson put it succinctly: this debate is about acting in the students' best interest, informed by the latest health advice.

Unions need to stop raising the white flag during this pandemic. Complaints about lack of hand sanitiser, student distancing or risks for older teachers can be solved with a little planning and innovation by administrators; the kind of agility the rest of the economy is showing through this crisis. Slamming the gate on children simply to cull attendance prevents that innovation from occurring.

During this lockdown, schools won't be full. That is thanks to parents with the skills to teach at home. As we have all conceded to home-schooling parents in the past, it is a feat much harder than we realised. Like trusting your family GP, parents prefer to entrust their child's learning to a teaching professional. A third of families are also paying fees throughout Covid-19 for the privilege. For these reasons, whatever the politics dictates, school is safe for children and we need to normalise attendance from next term.

Andrew Laming is a Liberal National MP, medical specialist and chairman of the federal Education Standing Committee.

Coronavirus: Time to run trials to find paths back to normal life
9 April 2020, *The Australian*

Just-released Covid-19 modelling would have been useful back in February, but not anymore. Australia's response can move on from the modelling of overrun hospital wards because, on current data, this simply won't happen.

What's more important is to understand the likely scale of this disease through the 2020 winter. The crucial measure is active cases; representing total infections less those recovered or succumbing. Active cases are heading for a manageable equilibrium, with infections brought in by travellers and cruise-ship passengers running their course while the ranks of the recovered increase.

So, the bigger question is which lockdown measures need to stay and which don't. The distant finish line is a vaccine early next year.

Like a high-stakes game of Jenga, there is no rule book on how and when to relax components of the response. Each working day of shutdown costs our GDP $1bn.

That is why the harder questions are how we minimise community transmission and which of our economic shutdowns are critical. This process will take time to test, so the sooner we start localised trials of restoring something like normal life, the better.

Australia's flattened Covid curve is both impressive and reassuring. Chinese research – published in *The Lancet* medical journal – describes six days from infection to the first symptoms, then a fork in the road 10 days later where around 10% of patients require more intensive care. By day 20, those cases have either recovered or succumbed. This allows reliable healthcare projections out to a three-week horizon.

The acceleration of new infections three weeks ago explains why our low death rates are suddenly rising. Despite that, our low rates of hospitalisation and use of intensive care units and ventilators remain world best.

We can be reassured by copious testing, with less than 2% found to be infected. It shows undiagnosed cases in the community are either uncommon or have little impact. That is supported by new cases of infections falling. If patients are initially refused a test and their condition worsens, they will return for testing, and a positive result goes into the data.

Some states were slow to report recovered cases, which muddied the waters and concealed an improving situation. Now that data has been updated, it will become clear from this week that the number of active cases are falling.

Thanks to contact tracing, we can separate out the infections originating on cruise ships and incoming aircraft and better understand the risk that remains. The spread of the virus in the community among those who did not travel is what Health Minister Greg Hunt is determined to prevent.

Promising falls in new cases over the past 10 days are due to a combination of lockdown measures, widespread and early detection, and possibly the weather being warmer than in much of the northern hemisphere.

As Deputy Chief Medical Officer Paul Kelly said, Australia is no Iran, Italy or Spain – meaning our experience of Covid-19 is likely to be less serious. Yet we can learn from other nations, especially those further advanced in the epidemic journey. Sweden, late to be affected and slow to shut down, now has 10 times our deaths. New Zealand jumped to complete shutdown, yet still its cases per million passed Australia's on Tuesday.

Queensland is the first state to see a viable path through winter emerging. With daily cases increasing just 1% a day recently, it is heading for a degree of stability with less than 1000 active cases overall. Total cases may reach 2000 but half will have already recovered by mid-June. Stress-testing our hospitals, if new infections were to double, ventilating about 20 patients at any one time is entirely manageable.

We can contrast Australia's 50 Covid-19 deaths so far with the 1255 flu deaths in 2017. Our hospital system can take heart if active cases stabilise around 6000. With 500 hospitalised at present, it is well short of the 13,500 flu admissions over the 2017 season.

While it is tempting to sit on the ice floe like penguins fearing the re-emergence of the killer whale, the only way to understand how to deal with the next stage of Covid-19 is for public health experts to cautiously trial local relaxations. Physical distancing and isolation costs less than the closure of business and can be monitored long-term. Economic shutdowns cost a fortune, so their public health benefit needs to be verified.

Just as states have a hotspot strategy for additional lockdowns, national cabinet needs to carefully trial the unlocking of "cooler spots" well away from areas of high caseloads. Stress-testing our response carries mortal risks. That is why we need closely monitored regional relaxations, fully supported from the top level of political leadership and clearly explained in regular media addresses.

With supply lines for personal protective items recovering, these can now be more liberally deployed in the workforce, particularly in areas that may be reopened. Since hair salons are still operating, these more relaxed rules could be extended to personal therapies, massage and yoga.

Childcare is open, so by extension play centres could be reopened. The activity of small group visual arts can extend to live-streamed orchestras and entertainment productions. Spacing rules in retail can be applied to reopen gyms and smaller dining venues. Hospitals with adequate emergency supplies should return to normal operations, knowing they can switch to Covid work within hours. Isolating the aged and frail, and the bans on larger congregations and non-essential travel, will all remain for some time yet.

This disease will be endemic for longer than we can lock down – either economically or psychologically. That is why maintaining hope and direction is vital. We need to stick with the cheap stuff that works and progressively shed the costly measures that may not be contributing much.

Scott Morrison will eventually outline the steps which will lead us out of the dark basement of isolation. Evoking Easter as resurrection, it is our economy that must eventually be brought back to life. That must begin with small steps — and as soon as possible.

Andrew Laming is a medical specialist, former infectious disease researcher and Queensland Coalition MP

Premiers and the Prime Minister need to put jobs first and reopen the service sector

2 May 2020, *Sydney Morning Herald*

States are taking cautious steps to unwind their Covid-19 lockdowns this weekend and the Prime Minister has flagged lifting restrictions on sport, business and social activity sooner rather than later. Re-employment, not recreation, must be the priority in this wind back effort. All states should be looking to re-start their service economies and reducing the economic blow the epidemic has inflicted.

Going into lockdown, Australia implemented a rugby scrum of measures, based on what we knew of Covid-19 at the time, plus lashings of precautionary principle. The path out is now better illuminated, thanks to a torrent of published data and information from our own lockdown. The virus is still in the rear-vision mirror but the economic clock is also ticking.

We can draw lessons from nations like Taiwan and Sweden that kept their economies running. Taiwan has recorded less than a tenth of Australia's Covid cases and only six deaths. Sweden also kept schools and workplaces open as well as allowing gatherings up to 50 people. This leaves Taiwan and Sweden in far better economic shape than their locked-down neighbours, although Sweden was unable to avoid more than 2600 deaths.

New Zealand in contrast, relied on harsher lockdowns to avert what was tracking to be a far worse epidemic than Australia. The true economic damage to the Tasman partners will be measured by inflation, productivity and domestic product levels years from now.

On global comparison, Australia occupies a Goldilocks zone, with wages falling less than 10% in early April and total deaths around 100. But of the price we have paid, much has fallen on the shoulders of around a million Australian service sector workers.

Impacted was not only travel and major events, but smaller operations capable of safe distancing, like dining and hospitality, complementary health, massage and myotherapy, nail and beauty, tattoo shops, art, dance and swim schools, gyms, yoga, physical trainers, plus the suppliers reliant upon them. In the end, allowing 67,000 hairdressers to trade was a propitious call; not a single case was traced to a salon.

That domestic evidence supports the Prime Minister's move for Covid-safe workplaces and industry-specific workplace health and safety guidelines. Once a premises meets distancing, hygiene and sanitation criteria, it is time to switch them back on.

Our public health experts must be cautious; they hold the lives of every Australian in their hands. But a million livelihoods are also on hold, with workers languishing at home based more on precaution than evidence. That is where politicians can now replace the precautionary principle with the cost-benefit of returning to work.

With Canberra bearing the brunt of JobKeeper and Jobseeker payments, states appear beset by moral hazard and in little rush to restart their economies.

This fragmentation will test national cabinet because the economic considerations simply can't penetrate the public health advice. This must become the Prime Minister's new priority because every working day lost is a billion dollars of GDP up in smoke. Every day lost makes the climb back to recovery even steeper.

Four facts have underpin the case for relaxation: First, Easter 2020 showed that extra activity didn't have an impact. Second, community testing is finding active disease minuscule. Third, the number of Covid-19 patients in the nation's ICUs is well under clinical capacity. Last, north-west Tasmania's outbreak was contained in just 12 days; proving that even in a regional and disadvantaged community, a second wave can be successfully managed.

These trends and the fact that most states have recorded 14 days without domestically acquired disease of unknown origin mean businesses should be opening tomorrow.

Just as schools are safe for children, service workplaces with appropriate social distancing are safe to reopen. While congregation and international travel is out, opening these micro and small businesses will set the platform for domestic travel, aviation and tourism in the next fortnight.

Australia's service sector is far from non-essential. The best way to pay back the Covid repair bill is to restart economic activity and get back to work.

Andrew Laming is a Liberal National MP, medical specialist and chairman of the federal Education Standing Committee.

Australia, you're ready for take-off if not for the premiers in ground control

6 September 2020, *Sydney Morning Herald*

Australia's golden ticket out of Covid-19 may well be international students. But to capitalise, premiers need to drop their airport arrival caps – and fast.

About a quarter of the $150 billion economic impact of international education flows to Australia. The remainder is captured by the United States, Britain and Canada but the lot is up for grabs for the first-mover nation that establishes a safe arrival model for students.

Unlike other parts of the economy, global students won't stop seeking qualifications. Australia needs to decide if it wants to meet that market. At present we are the laggard.

We are also the only nation worldwide that limits our citizens returning. Set by paranoid premiers who jumped the Prime Minister in early July, these caps on arrivals from overseas were a panicked response to Victoria's self-inflicted second wave of the virus. Astoundingly, the limits were arbitrarily extended to 24 October with barely a whimper.

South Australian Premier Steven Marshall will trial accepting 300 international students. It is a flicker of sanity among premiers who otherwise see a single case of Covid as a political catastrophe. It isn't.

Gladys Berejiklian is proof so far that sensible suppression and light-touch lockdown can navigate a huge state economy through the Covid abyss.

Limiting arrivals to 500 a week is the most egregious distortion of the science so far. All states but Victoria proved hotel quarantine is safe. But we carry on with near-empty hotels and their staff languishing on JobKeeper when they should be able to embrace their "new normal" thanks to a restarting of international travel.

Instead, premiers wallow in moral hazard, knowing the economic damage of their overreaction is underwritten by Canberra.

As the clock ticks towards a new academic year, the national cabinet needs to increase repatriation of Australian citizens to 1000 a day and clear this backlog by the end of September.

That could position the nation to welcome back the 900,000 international students, plus more who may seek to avoid countries where Covid is out of control. Skilled workers and their families will also need a arrival mechanism.

Of course, Australia can rise to this challenge. Brisbane alone has 5 million hotel bed nights annually and the Gold Coast half that number again. Currently Premier Annastacia Palaszczuk quarantines just 50 people a day while the remainder of Queensland's accommodation sector is on its knees, wallowing in JobKeeper payments.

If our federation was as strong as it should be, Queensland would shoulder a little extra airport burden to take the strain off Victoria. Sadly, it wasn't written into the AFL grand final relocation deal.

Worse, airport caps force Australians to pay as much as $20,000 to return on a near-empty flight and wait until January 2021. This week's Commonwealth loans to stranded overseas citizens risk going straight into the pockets of grateful Middle Eastern airline owners.

Locking down south-east Queensland due to two cases of coronavirus a day is all about milking Covid through to a state election. These policies departed the solar system of reasonable science months ago.

The news media reports state border overreaction but seems to miss the bigger picture: the billion-dollar losses we face if we can't sort out international travel.

Quarantining, transferring and feeding arrivals into hotel rooms is among the simplest public policy challenge imaginable. Failing that elementary test, Victorian Premier Daniel Andrews' second wave has now doubled the nation's lockdown time and cost, tripled the Covid cases and sextupled the deaths. But even that blunder is not grounds for overreaction by other states.

Removing airport caps would allow flights to operate efficiently and ticket prices to plummet. International freight costs could normalise and loans to those languishing overseas would instead help pay hotel quarantine costs.

Domestic tourism is only a small fraction of our $60 billion tourism industry. That is why international movement and associated quarantine is one of the few glimmers of hope for our 500,000 urban hotel and catering workers.

Currently, airport policies are the bottleneck, strangling the most JobKeeper-reliant sector we have. Broadscale hotel quarantine is precisely how we can live with Covid, rather than in fear of it.

Almost a million international students are right now asking Australian education institutions if they are ready to do business. That $37 billion of economic activity offers us the only lifeline to start paying our way out of the Covid mess.

4

health

How to prune Australia's $5 Billion pill-popping tab

15 April 2005, *The Age*

Australians are paying far too much for generic drug replacements, writes Andrew Laming.

Fifty years ago, the Pharmaceutical Benefits Scheme was created to deliver essential drugs affordably. As a small economy, Australia secured new patented drugs by locking them at an agreed price. In return, overseas drug firms gained certainty and market penetration in GPs' surgeries nationwide.

So why is our PBS growing four times faster than the economy? Why has it become a behemoth that pays out more than $5 billion a year to foreign drug companies? And why, in a generation, will it consume $1 in every $28 of the Australian economy?

To the surprise of many, the novel and expensive new drugs are not the culprits. In fact, new drugs are 47% cheaper here than in the US. Nor can we blame our ageing population, our prescription culture or the PBS proliferation to more than 1500 products because those conditions exist worldwide.

The key threat to our PBS is internal; a simple design flaw, which leaves us paying top price for generic drugs, the very products that are right now reducing drug costs in other countries.

That fatal flaw is a suicide gene for the PBS. Like all leading economies, Australia rewards innovative drug firms with 20 years of patent protection. Back in the 1950s, the PBS never foresaw the need to lower prices for expensive drugs when they finally came off patent. That leaves the PBS helpless.

Consider a common depression medicine for which New Zealand pays $1.45 and Britain $4.97 per month per patient. Here we pay $33.03 because there is no mechanism to reduce prices below the PBS set price for the branded equivalent.

This generic loophole actually undermines the great deals we strike for new drugs. Worse still, Australia rewards the drug copycats at the expense of the firms that do the high-risk research for break-through drugs. It stands to reason that the only way we can afford breakthrough drugs is to stop paying top dollar when patents expire.

It wasn't that long ago that everyone was encouraged to substitute expensive drugs with generic alternatives. Most US health services and many of our medical schools and public hospitals mandate the use of generics. But in Australia's private sector, switching to a generic is pointless because in most cases it helps neither the patient nor the taxpayer. The generic market is so lucrative that innovator firms actually make generics to compete against themselves.

Those big profit margins allow generic firms to spread the largesse along the supply chain. In addition to courting doctors, generics offer sizeable discounts to pharmacists, meaning few savings are passed on to the taxpayer or patient. Doctors in turn have little incentive to prescribe generics and patients no reason to ask for them. Little wonder that generics have fallen to only 19% of Australian prescriptions, compared with more than 50% in Denmark, Germany, Britain and Canada.

Rather than rolling over and playing dead, our revered PBS needs a dose of Viagra to get generic prices on par with international prices of between $2 and $15 a month.

Reintroducing competition won't be easy but it can be done. Health Minister Tony Abbott moved in the right direction recently, achieving more competition with a 12.5% discount agreement. This cut creates a lower ceiling price but won't achieve the subsequent price cuts that are so dearly needed.

There is a solution, and it starts with removing generic drugs from the PBS. As post-patent copy drugs, they have no right to a free ride on prices set for their patented equivalents. Generics would be priced according to patient demand, just like vitamins and toiletries.

Generic firms face two choices. Some may leave the Australian market, though this is unlikely given the low prices they accept overseas. More likely, they will set their prices just under the present PBS co-payment of $28.60. Anything above this and patients would stick with brand-name drugs. This policy will lead to generics having two shelf prices, depending on whether or not patients have concession cards.

Generics costing more than the $28.60 co-payment would no longer receive any government transfers. Most of these products are cheaper than $28.60 in other OECD nations and could be expected to fall. Drugs between $28.60 and the concession price of $4.60 would remain unchanged for those without concession cards, but fall to $4.60 for concessionaire scripts. Any higher and patients would return to branded products.

Lastly, the few affordable generics under $4.60 would be unaffected by the policy.

The second step is to negotiate with manufacturers a rebate for each prescription to keep generics on Australian shelves. Generic firms would negotiate with the Government a rebate for each drug family where a generic is available.

With each drug family, a Dutch auction would set the lowest possible rebate to keep a generic option in the market. A small bonus would be paid to the first generic firm to accept the offer. Unlike New Zealand's draconian system, competition would be maintained because all generics, not just the lowest bidder, could remain in the marketplace. This rebate is independent of the PBS price and certain to be considerably cheaper.

In most cases, a $5 subsidy, plus the patient co-payment, would be enough to keep most generics on the shelves. The final step is to offer a small co-payment reduction on generics. This is a potent demand driver, particularly among concessionaires and should be used if the generic sector fails to grow. No solution will keep everyone happy, but a billion dollars saved annually will pay for lifesaving new drugs and preserve the PBS for our children.

Andrew Laming is an ophthalmic surgeon and the Liberal MHR for Bowman

Queensland Doctor Crisis

20 January 2006, *The Courier Mail*

Facing a doctor crisis like never before, Queensland Health will be forced to shut down services or close hospitals in 2006, writes Andrew Laming.

Today's incentives for rural health workers announced by Federal Health Minister Tony Abbott are revolutionary but not enough to save a Queensland health system in crisis. Rural GPs offering surgical, anaesthetic and obstetric services in local hospitals are now entitled to annual $15,000 practice incentives. Australia's remote procedural doctors were almost obliterated by overwork and the 2002 indemnity crisis. Massive cash transfers aim to retain the current crop and lure new recruits west.

At the same time, remote nurses, midwives and Aboriginal health workers will receive Medicare rebates for pregnancy checks on behalf of a doctor. Offering Medicare to allied health workers shares the clinical load in remote areas, is a major shift in Australia's medico-centric system.

Solutions for our health system need two Governments working together. The Commonwealth runs Medicare rebates and pharmaceuticals, retaining control over number of providers volume and rebates price. In contrast, our free public hospitals can only control costs by cutting volume. That's why delays in emergency departments, dental hospitals and surgical waiting lists are no accident. Just last year Tony Abbott restored bulk-billing levels by raising doctors' rebates. Now Queensland must achieve similar heroics in its public hospitals.

Unfortunately for Queensland, workforce solutions are more complex than merely raising rebates. Queensland Health is a chronic under-spender; $300 per person less than south of the border. Worse, they explained it away as being more efficient!

Closer scrutiny shows how flawed that thinking was. Despite our decentralisation, Queensland employs fewer hospital staff than any mainland state, fewer nurses, fewer ancillary staff and together with WA, the fewest doctors. With 22% fewer nurses per person than Victoria, emerging 'Jayant Patel' incidents are less likely to be detected early.

Queensland Health planners discovered that if the service was slow enough, hospital use would fall. While Australian figures were unchanged, Queensland attendance went into free-fall; from 212 to 193 per 1000 persons over three years. Queensland's emergency departments have slipped to seeing just 60% of patients in a timely manner. Similarly, far fewer people receive an operation within 'a clinically appropriate time frame.'

Balancing workforce, technology and utilization is the challenge in health care. After a decade of Queensland cost-cutting, mapping a way out of the abyss won't be easy, with the sceptre of Dr Death haunting every recruitment drive. Politicians criticising overseas-trained doctors aggravates the situation, because it verges on racism and dissuades excellent clinicians from applying. With the right medical training, overseas doctors with adequate supervision are a vital part of all developed health systems, which use remuneration, training and lifestyle to recruit. Right now, too many other parts of the world have more attractive health systems than Queensland.

Turning that around is a major planning and public relations exercise. Premier Beattie's overhaul of medical registration has left the Board in utter crisis, highlighting the lunacy of a small nation sustaining eight differing medical registration systems. Southern states are now poaching our potential new recruits. Like a train wreck in slow motion, the implications of old policy are only now becoming apparent. The short-term crisis is to avoid lives being lost in the carriages which are careering into the policy errors of previous years. But such a focus shouldn't obscure the need for long-term solutions.

Queensland Health is deckchair-shuffling by moving bureaucrats out of Charlotte St. Their old habits have returned, with up-front hospital charges contemplated, which further undermines access. Health Minister Robertson's demand for a more 'efficient, prompt and welcoming' Medical Board is five years too late, because consecutive recruitment drives have failed and recruiting a doctor can take well over 12 months.

As Acting Premier Anna Bligh is surely receiving secret briefings on closing hospitals and wards, the big cash injections delivered years too late are suddenly looking impotent. Managing health workforce isn't rocket science; so long as your system isn't the worst of the bunch. With that mantle conferred, Queensland will be into innovative cost-shifting, high-cost locums and expanded after hours deputising services to avoid collapse.

Home birthing: the fiscal nips and tucks to our health system

21 September 2009, *Online Opinion*

As former MP Danna Vale said, all politics is not just local, but personal. Just a fraction of Australians elect to birth at home but the fervour of those that do can be evangelical. In Canberra's grey rain this week, 2,000 devoted mums and midwives won a two-year reprieve from being deregistered and fined if they attend a home birth.

But there were few cheers for Minister Roxon's back flip. Landmark reform stemming from the recent National Maternity Services Review proposes autonomy for midwives around prescribing certain drugs and ordering tests as well as long awaited access to Medicare and indemnity cover. But for home birthing midwives, neither Medicare support nor any form of indemnity protection is on offer.

When it comes to the safety of low-risk mums birthing at home, the world's foremost medical evidence authority is the Cochrane Collaboration. With appropriate hospital support says Cochrane, home birth and hospital mortality for low-risk bubs is comparable.

The Cochrane global evidence base supports women having a right to choose between the two options. They acknowledge that outcomes for mums may actually be worse in hospitals. The largest of all studies was a nationwide cohort of 529,688 low-risk planned home and hospital births by de Jonge in the Netherlands. It found that "planning a homebirth does not increase the risks of perinatal mortality and severe perinatal morbidity among low-risk women, provided the maternity care system facilitates this choice through the availability of well-trained midwives and through a good transportation and referral system".

For many mums, the traumatic hospital experience is the centrifugal force pulling hundreds away from anodyne medical wards and back to home. Midwives have followed, disenchanted by the "clock-in clock-out" hospital work and the constant turnover of care. They see hospitals as fragmented, overly medical and homebirth as a relationship-based approach. The cascade of hospital interference includes needles and gas, probes and clips through to forceps, extractors and ultimately caesarean section. Not to suggest these interventions are unnecessary; simply overapplied.

For most of us, these gadgets are part of the safe baby experience; the community expectation that every baby arrives in perfect health. But we also accept over-intervention, infections and medical side-effects as unavoidable.

Home birthers are rankled by any suggestion that they would ever subject their babies to any undue risks by delivering at home and believe massive nation-wide cohort studies back their claims.

Less acknowledged is that home births exert a counter-pressure upon our hospital system. Birth plans, continuity of care, the demand for fewer interventions and the reemphasis upon emotional attachment to mums are all hospital trends originating from the home birthing phenomenon. Few realise that the emerging threats to home birthing have more to do with the global financial crisis than any bigotry, intolerance or obstetricians.

Late last year, flawed Treasury modelling prescribed a ridiculously large stimulus which threw Australia into debt faster than any other country. Like all resource exporters, our economy barely stumbled, but it's too late to recover the cash. Now it's up to Treasury to claw back the balance sheet. From alcopops and cataracts to IVF and pathology, our health system is paying the price for the ill-disciplined spending elsewhere.

Until now the fiscal nips and tucks to our health system have been politically painless. Taxing alcohol drew public health support, pathologists are mostly corporate and cataract surgeons far too wealthy to arouse public sympathy in any case. Conception however is the most incendiary moral issue in medicine and our elected officials are about to learn birthing isn't far behind. Australians rarely march in the streets; certainly not for blood tests or eye operations. But mums choosing home births do so in the context of historical resistance to their choices.

The Health Minister understands that extending indemnity cover to include community midwifery will come at a cost. It may only be 0.5% of women who deliver at home, but actuarial analysis is complicated by the infrequency of intranatal misadventure and the potential for million-dollar payouts. Those calculations deserve to be performed, and insurers allowed to work with the sector to agree on how insurance can be made available.

The Health Minister's two-year moratorium is a brief reprieve before home birthing again becomes illegal. Bad policy in two years is still bad policy. Its one thing to decimate home birthing by setting up an exclusive "registration" club for midwives which excommunicates those attending home births. It is an even greater affront to fine them. Such an approach will draw quality mainstream midwives out of home birthing and imperil safety.

The Minister would be far better advised to draw midwifery together under a single maternity care system of registration, indemnity and support. Home birthing will never disappear; we owe our mums and their babies a comprehensive system which recognises, insures and drives high quality maternity in hospital and at home. In this regard, Australia need only look to New Zealand for a two-decade track record of integrated community midwifery.

Rudd's haste on health risks making things worse

27 April 2010, *Online Opinion*

Many of us have forgotten to do our homework then cobbled a paper together the day before it's due. It may work occasionally for teenagers and university students but it isn't acceptable for a Prime Minister tackling something as important as health reform.

Kevin Rudd had promised to fix Australia's hospital system last year but got distracted. He then burned through $100 billion worth of stimulus, which completely neglected health care. Now just a few months out from another election it has suddenly become his number one priority. So much so that he pretty much refuses to talk about anything else. Faced with the trifecta of global warming, people smugglers and hospitals which could all derail his prime ministership, the Prime Minister chose the only one which can be fixed with cash; and lots of it.

For a Prime Minister intoxicated with inputs instead of outcomes, money is all that matters. While Australia's $100 billion health system is in line with those in other rich nations at around $5,000 per person annually, it is without doubt one of the most complex because it involves a precarious balancing act of the private and public sectors.

We have a $30 billion hospital system where the more work they do the faster they go broke. Then there is a $20 billion Medicare service where the faster you work the more you get paid. These two systems actively repel work back at each other - hospitals by understaffing and Medicare because GPs need to sleep at night. A third of our system is private, delivering efficient but selected services for the insured. That leaves 75,000 bureaucrats in eight different public health systems keen to keep their jobs and maintain the status quo.

Rudd's solution is more a government shake-up than genuine health reform. First there is the pea and thimble trick where the Commonwealth takes 30% of GST then hands it to regional health bureaucracies. Second, there will be some standardisation of processes with incentives for efficient hospital services. Last and most important, money will be targeting the three key fault lines in health; casualty delays, waiting lists and bed block.

However, amidst the haste there have been glaring omissions. Rudd's plan contains no provision for mental health and none for the widely rorted dental items. Further, Rudd's plan makes no provision for independent reporting on the hospital performance. What's needed is an independent watchdog. Not government appointees and spin doctors paid to hide the truth. Rudd knows states will never agree to any independent scrutiny, so he hasn't proposed it.

Clinically, we need to prevent hospitals shifting their costs back onto Medicare. But Rudd provides states with more money to continue the overlap and duplication. Hospitals need incentives to do more of what they do best like specialist outpatient services. Instead, those programs are being closed down to save money.

We need to support private health, but Mr Rudd undermines insured Australians by fast-tracking desperate public patients into private hospitals. Australia needs a single funder, but Rudd's scheme keeps two. We need public and private providers competing to deliver services but that won't happen either. Telecare monitoring of the frail at home could prevent expensive admissions, but Rudd has run out of time. A unique patient identifier could unify health records nationwide and save millions. Same story.

Our hospitals are crying out for some outside governance like local hospital boards. Rudd's proposal simply splits up the existing bureaucracies and adds a fourth level; regional health boards, so named because Tony Abbott's local boards plan proved popular. When a region inevitably goes broke, Rudd has created three separate administrations who can blame each other, and more bureaucrats to manage the triple interface. Come election day, voters will have no idea who to blame.

As Queensland's head bureaucrat, Rudd had little passion for health reform. That's partly explains Queensland Health now. It also explains the rush. He is talking big health reform yet spent the last three weeks cutting ribbons on cancer machines in marginal seats instead of the harder task of cutting red tape.

Long after the memories of Rudd slaying the Premiers have faded, patients will still languish in casualty departments, seniors will be stuck in hospital beds and waiting lists will remain just that. For sure many of Rudd's ideas are good, because there are good people giving him the ideas. But the haste for a pre-election solution risks making our already complex system even more bloated and no less wasteful.

Our woes are just beginning

13 January 2011, *The Age*

These catastrophic floods have set in motion a series of serious health problems across Queensland.

In what is likely to be Australia's worst natural disaster, an area the size of Victoria is now flooded between Rockhampton and Brisbane, putting a strain on the resources of Queensland's health services. Storm cells can be tracked but predicting when and in which catchments falls will occur remains imprecise. These floods have simultaneously blocked air and land access to affected areas at various times, delaying the redeployment of our most capable first responders to the areas where they are needed most.

The health challenges vary across Queensland. In the Fitzroy River basin last week, flood levels silently rose over the sandbags, drowned the pumps and inundated GP practices. There was no option but to evacuate. In the Lockyer and Toowoomba storm cell on Monday, flash floods came and went within two hours. In Grantham and Helidon, bodies remained unrecoverable yesterday, allowing time for Toowoomba to expand its mortuary capacity to 24 places if required.

Our world-class health infrastructure is struggling to cope.

SMS alerts were the great lesson from the 2009 Victorian bushfires, yet they haven't been implemented across Queensland. Nor have we acquired the helicopter extraction platforms that airlift entire families off a roof.

Local emergency committees are run by councils, but many have been slow to respond to threats outside their boundaries. That has frustrated health, ambulance, fire and police units, which have statewide co-ordination.

Across the state, flood-related health challenges include access to safe drinking water, medicine and hygienic food. Rockhampton is managing an outbreak of food poisoning due to food and water contamination, compounded by the sub-tropical climate and power interruption. For 24 hours Toowoomba residents boiled water while repairs were made.

Of the diarrhoeal diseases, the most dreaded are staphylococcal endotoxins, leading to severe food poisoning, toxic shock or lung disease if inspired. Relief workers may require respirators, given that endotoxins reached 20 times normal levels in homes after Hurricane Katrina. Cholera can also cause fatal dehydration. None of this is helped by the fact that rural people are notoriously stoic and reluctant to trouble others with their problems.

In western Queensland, wounds risk becoming infected and existing chronic illness exacerbated. Rather than physical trauma, the main symptom bringing people to Toowoomba hospital has been stress-related chest pain. Insect-born disease is inevitable, but it varies across these large affected areas.

Inland, St George is submerged in a sand fly epidemic. Rockhampton is within the southern extent of dengue fever range. Inland, mosquito-borne diseases like Ross River chronic arthritis will have even higher prevalence and potentially an earlier outbreak, depending on how many of the breeding sites were washed away in the initial flood surge. Right now there will be severe infectious illnesses of unknown cause being managed in major hospitals down the east coast.

Moulds grow in carpets and walls within 48 hours. Damp indoor spaces can persist for weeks, threatening residents and remediation workers. Spores aggravate allergies and severe asthma attacks in children and rare conditions such as aspergillosis in the frail. Moulds also contaminate foods that might have otherwise avoided floodwater contact.

Alternative power sources such as generators, lanterns and gas ranges inside homes run the risk of carbon monoxide poisoning. At agreed flood levels, Queensland towns shut down utilities such as power, water and sewage services. Levied towns fill stormwater drains with earth to prevent backflow into town centres. Even loos are sandbagged to prevent sewage backflow. Residents return to discover homes and livelihoods sodden with toxic water, sewage, animal and human faeces and petroleum products. Flooding in rural centres around Toowoomba present additional challenges such as pesticides, herbicides, destroyed crops and dead livestock.

All these challenges are aggravated by rural health workforce shortages and damaged supply lines. Floods have isolated families from essential pharmaceuticals. In Rockhampton, drug wholesaler Sigma is using watercraft to deliver essentials to Gracemere from which rural pharmacies and hospitals can be supplied.

Medical consumables including bottled oxygen have been in short supply. Inland from Rockhampton, general anaesthesia capacity is severely limited and employed judiciously.

Native and domesticated fauna are also on the move. Stray dog bites were the No. 1 challenge in St George, particularly for rescue workers entering private property. Parents most fear venomous snakes escaping rising waters and swimming into and under their homes. Exposure to rats also presents slight risks of diseases like leptospirosis.

For all the talk of being a resilient people, mental and psychological illness will quietly devastate families without ever making the evening news. This will affect the relief workers themselves. A tough environment and natural disasters can never inoculate us from the anxiety, depression and hopelessness of losing loved ones, friends, life savings and livelihoods. Nor are our children spared.

This horrific event is likely to compound the long-standing depression and anxiety inevitable in communities supporting barely viable rural businesses in tough economic times. Everyone prayed for rain, but no one dreamt of this.

Coaches to coax better health outcomes

7 February 2011, *Online Opinion*

Everyone has been part of a flippant conversation about life expectancy. It ends with the inevitable shrug and acknowledgement that when it happens it happens. In reality, most of us set our own date, by making daily diet and lifestyle choices with life-long consequences.

Apart from the quarter of us who succumb to injuries, accidents, mental health issues or rare diseases, it's the way we eat and exercise that determines the quality and duration of our lives.

So given that almost all of us can afford to eat well and stay fit, it's important to understand why so many of us exchange great health for inactivity and unhealthy food.

Behavioural experts remind us that short term pleasures trump delayed gratification. The best example is the rush experienced with smoking. There is no greater predictor of bad health than cigarettes.

Talk to any person struggling with their health and they will single out motivation as the key. Australia's fee-for-service system delivers over eight GP visits and nine prescriptions per Australian per year.

But even that is failing to motivate enough of us to lose the girth, the kilos, unclog our arteries and control our blood pressure.

We also know that around nine million Australians don't fully comprehend health advice, medical information and discussions with clinicians. Mainstream health providers have so far struggled to get messages through to those with low levels of health literacy.

Ultimately, the State hospital systems pick up the tab for bad health choices and the poor understanding which underpins it. They battle both the moral hazard that health expenses are ultimately paid by others and the adverse selection which leaves the sickest patients in the public system.

Economists are a dry lot; often joking that it is not when you die, but how that matters. Dying quick and cheap saves the system, while slow debilitating conditions requiring intensive support throw our health budgets into overdrive.

Private health insurers know this too. They are in the business of finding ways to intervene in this cycle of decline. They know that beating bad health is equally about living longer and dying cheaper. Keeping your mobility and avoiding hideously expensive cardiac operations are good examples.

Short of financially punishing bad health choices with larger gaps, higher fees or fines, health planners are desperate to develop new carrots to drive healthy behaviour however they can.

Now, insurers and State governments are hiring third parties to do the extra coaching.

Connecting Care supports those most likely to end in hospital with positive behaviour change. That includes education, guidance and support to reinforce the health recommendations so often ignored as we walk home from the doctors.

Telephonic health coaching – literally phone-based training – is one way to tailor the health message to individual levels of health literacy. That builds a fuller understanding of the health message, and alerts patients to what they can do to change outcomes. It also delivers these things at a much lower economic and time cost than face to face consultations.

NSW Health announced this week the contracting of one such firm to phone coach around 36,000 people with chronic and complex needs. These are the people with serious conditions who without urgent intervention are highly likely to end up back in hospital.

Brief but frequent interventions are one way to head off unhealthy practices between hospital visits and to identify problems early. Those in this first phone coaching group include patients with diabetes, high blood pressure, heart and lung disease.

We all talk up health promotion, but few in the business know what reliably works. Government-sponsored TV ads are politically popular but cost millions without any guarantee they alter behaviour. Agrawal and Duhachek identified defensive processing as one reason why.

The April 2010 *Journal of Marketing Research* reported that ads led to defensive processing where individuals assessed their personal circumstances as better than those portrayed in the ads. Put simply, we view our own personal greatness as a buffer from potential negative consequence, whether it's drink-driving, smoking or eating junk food.

Clearly, we need a more intensive approach which connects ill-health to actions. Health coaching can be evaluated, by examining comparable groups which aren't coached. Early results published in the *Population Health Management* magazine found health coached groups were 20% less likely to be admitted to hospitals.

Health coaches cost less than doctors and they can reach more people more often using phone and computerised interventions. More detailed studies will tease out which sub-groups respond best to counselling and why.

As free agents, we should be left to our own lifestyle choices. But the will of responsible people to invest in expensive remedies for people who consciously elect to be unhealthy is not unlimited.

The price of bad lifestyle is deferred but it is always ultimately paid in full. Part of the challenge for government is to better align cause and effect. Only by paying the true price of unhealthy lifestyle now will individuals decide the price isn't worth it.

Personal health coaches aren't cheap but against a backdrop of exponentially increasing healthcare costs, the potential money and lives saved could be dramatic.

Labor no closer to the big answers in health care

April 2011, *Australian Polity*, Volume 2, Number 1.

The older we get, the more we think about our health. By the time we get there, it is too late to change the system. Health is arguably the most complex policy area of all. That is because social preconditions like equity, rights and the value of life run constant interference on market economics.

Technology rejected as too expensive elsewhere is demanded in health care. Market failure and irrationality are constant companions for health planners, as they battle powerful human expectations like survival instinct, compassion and greed. Moral hazard and adverse selection in Australia's welfare system further tests our ability to drive improvements in disability adjusted life-years within existing budget allocations.

Moral hazard rewards ignoring health until we cannot be saved. Adverse selection drives the worried well to private insurance and the rest to be picked up by public hospitals. Australia incubates health inefficiencies in the name of universality. We lack the co-payment and deductible components which work to drive health need to appropriate services.

Worldwide, lead economies are reforming their health systems. That is no reason for Australia to, but it never hurts to pick over good ideas which complement the best elements of our own.

At primary care level, our understanding of behavioural change around chronic disease remains limited, to the point that investment methodologies remain uncertain. At the high-tech end of both pharmaceutical and interventional medicine, purchasing and provision remains inefficient with patients using patented drugs and treatments when cheaper options offer equivalent outcomes. Both areas have been ignored by federal Labor, which remains preoccupied with organizational reform. Finally, it is argued that while stakeholder support is vital, community support is the only precondition sufficient to guarantee change.

Australia's first challenge is that two% of us consume half the health budget. While healthy, we average three General Practitioner visits a year, with fees paid for service rather than outcome. There are no special arrangements when these briefest of interventions fail to arrest weight gain, blood pressure, cholesterol, or blood sugar.

As a result of long lags between lifestyle choices and health outcomes, Governments and private health insurers are compelled pick up the tab. They have little say in when, where or how often that occurs. Insurers often do not even realise their client has a chronic disease until the bill arrives for an emergency admission or operation. Massive benefits exist if the 98% of us who are 'well' worked with insurers rather than using them as somewhere to send invoices. Currently legislation prevents that from happening.

Despite us all agreeing prevention trumps curative medicine, the financial demands of Medicare and state-run hospitals crowd out adequate funding for each of the three tiers of preventative health: tertiary prevention focuses on chronic disease patients, secondary prevention focuses on stabilizing at-risk groups and primary prevention includes public health messaging.

Australia has embarked on a bipartisan Close the Gap strategy but it needs a second one. The seven-year rural longevity gap has for too long been regarded as 'part of living in the bush.' Currently, Government drives supply side workforce solutions hoping bonuses, more graduates and overseas trainees will deliver the workforce. But trickling them out using relocation and remoteness bonuses will be a slow and expensive process.

A better alternative is to directly engage health bodies to spread the rural service obligation across their professions, using tradable units that individuals can either deliver or pay others to. Urban practices could form sibling arrangements to serve rural patients online or in person. Providers unwilling to serve postcodes outside cities would simply pay for the privilege, by trading the time to others who will.

Urban hospitals would also partner with remote regions. Departments would back fill hospital positions starting 'remote-first.' This means the urban health workforce would pool responsibility for their rural and remote areas. Urban job descriptions would incorporate modest amounts of regional service. Dentistry and medical specialties may consider post-qualification internships as well as semi-supervised rural placements post-fellowship. Precisely deployed three to six month terms for these future graduates would mostly eliminate vacancies in rural Australia. Professional clinical groups would have a key role in either filling these posts or advocating for expanded trainee numbers.

In the process, rural hospitals will have to rise to the challenge of activity-based funding. It may sound simplistic, but hospital funding should be based on the services they provide, with funding adjustments if necessary. Rather than abandon support for a national pricing authority, New South Wales and Queensland should negotiate additional time to build hospital competitiveness, given the state of their systems after two decades of Labor decline.

As primary health care strengthens, role substitution will see practitioners working under the supervision of General Practitioners to keep Australians out of hospitals and away from their General Practitioners. In fact, General Practitioners may accrue bonuses for the proportion of care they drive into multi-disciplinary teams.

Labor's insistence on the term Medicare Local suggests they are now only one step away from allocating Medicare notionally to local regions. This would cap item number activity in certain areas and raise the incentive to shift effort to poorer and underserved areas with unused Medicare budgets.

The Dutch transformed their health system in 2006 to a universal private insurance model, incorporating subsidised options for low income earners. Australians fear US-style health care, so any changes must first escape the accusation of 'dismantling Medicare.'

One method of increasing incentives in state hospitals to deliver services on time is to tender overdue public operating work to the private sector. Those waiting sixty days longer than recommended wait times would be tendered across region, state or even across state boundaries to be delivered by public or private operating lists with unused capacity. The Commonwealth would then bill laggard States for the Medicare component, a surgical bonus and inpatient stay costs. Such a policy shifts hospital focus from cost-minimisation to efficiency and provides a safety net for surgical patients.

But it also cuts the other way. The Commonwealth would meet the costs born by the states for the inpatient stays due to lack of a Commonwealth funded aged care place. This competitive mechanism at the margins would benefit patients by establishing financial rewards for timely and quality care. States should run transitional care because they are the beneficiaries of the savings. It also avoids State hospitals cost-shifting.

Newly elected Coalition State Governments will make cooperative federalism more complex, but not impossible. With dire budget positions at both Commonwealth and State levels, it is only Coalition Governments – with their focus on eliminating waste – that can guarantee a larger proportion of health expenditure reaches frontline patient care and preventative health, rather than the clip-board carriers and unionists who take a clip along the way.

Rudd spent the remainder of his crumbling administration rewriting GST agreements in order to redistribute state money to the Commonwealth. This was in the context of massive federal budget deficits. On top of this, state governments were well aware that health costs would soon outstrip the compensation on offer from Canberra. Unfortunately, those fumbling reforms plough on, even as Labor Governments disappear from the COAG table.

There are two behemoth challenges facing advanced health systems worldwide. Effective interventions to minimise lifestyle disease remain elusive and the new technology alternatives are increasingly unaffordable. These frontiers are yet to be even acknowledged by a Labor administration, increasingly fixated upon its own political survival.

Healthier population and budget

28 April 2011, *Online Opinion*

The global pharmaceutical industry is twice Australia's annual budget. Australians burn through their fair share of drugs, consuming nine billion dollars of allopathic and natural remedies annually. So it defies belief that to this day, over a third of prescriptions written simply don't work.

Efforts to genetically map health and disease have demonstrated just how complex the picture really is. Disease can be any number of genetically influenced processes which differ between individuals. It helps explain why most drugs work in some and not others. For the first time, tests can help to tell these patient groups apart, before we embark on treatment.

It is said doctors start their careers knowing a little about many drugs and end their careers knowing much about just a handful. In between, enormous sums are spent on ineffectual treatments. Now, thanks to genomics, all that could change.

This transformation is shifting effort from 'what works', to 'upon whom.' Welcome to the era of personalised medicine. Not just a personal doctor, but where treatments work specifically on you.

Just ten years ago, we were heading in precisely the opposite direction. Blockbuster drugs offered population-wide benefits to reduce blood pressure, lipids and obesity. These drugs were so promising, some joked they could be added to the water supply. Breaking the bank was collateral damage for governments to sort out.

Ultimately it got too expensive to measure these minor health improvements across broad populations. Since 2000, bringing a new treatment to market has blown out from $800 million to a staggering $1.3 billion. New drug applications to the US drug approving body FDA steadily fell as result, to around 25 annually.

Worst of all, many new drugs were falling at the last hurdle, with an overall 90% failure rate at the end of phase III human trials. That was often after huge sums had already been invested. The blockbusters appeared promising in animal studies but couldn't always establish their cost-efficacy in humans.

Government is shifting ground too. Tired of paying for drugs unleashed on whole populations, it's in their interest to identify precisely which patients are in the 40% for which prescriptions will fail due to personal variation. Approvers now demand evidence up front on who responds and why. In cancer treatment for instance, government is sick of paying for tumour shrinkage alone. It's now all about quality and duration of extra life. The new term is companion diagnosis; using accompanying biomarker tests to stratify patients into who responds, how well and who won't. The potential to eliminate inefficiency and waste in health systems is enormous.

Medical diagnosis will also be transformed. In the past broad disease categories like multiple sclerosis had complex clinical courses, with subsets of patients having vastly different outcomes. We are uncovering new connections between molecular level processes occurring across a range of diseases.

A deliciously named new treatment called canakinumab exemplifies this shift to molecular pathways. Initially used to treat a few thousand worldwide living with a rare autoimmune disease called CAPS, it has just been revealed that the same molecular process is at play in gout. Suddenly this rare treatment offers hope to three million worldwide struggling with a far more common affliction.

New prognostic and risk information can help us find the right drugs for the right patient. That allows subgroups to be monitored and prevented differently, saving our health systems millions of dollars. As companion diagnosis expands, Government will increasingly seek to remunerate not the drug, but the clinical result. Moving from rewarding transaction to outcomes will ultimately spread from pharmacology across the rest of health care. Genomics already assists with identifying which lymph node negative breast cancer patients will recover without additional chemotherapy. In this case genomics also tells us how to save $100 million a year by not treating. It's a test which more than pays for itself. It isn't much of a leap beyond here to adjust surgical payments according to their clinical outcomes.

Pharmacogenomics is still emerging. Major pharmaceutical companies have identified just a handful of biological pathways for intensive analysis. In 2011, there are around twenty FDA-listed products where prescribers are advised to gather genetic information prior to prescribing. An example is the third of heart attack or stroke patients who lack an enzyme and are therefore unable to respond to Lopidogril. The right test can save us 30% of total drug costs. On top of that we avoid the adverse reactions, the treatment delays, the extra patient consultations and inconvenience.

The days of fiddling with drug structure to extend its life in the market may be numbered. Genomics identifies drug targets, which in turn offers a host of new applications for molecules. Virtual and computational drug design can predict human toxicity long before we need to put compounds into animals or people. PET scans now allow us to image pharmaco-anatomy and witness drugs hitting their target. The immediate challenge is to identify the most likely candidates for intensive development from countless opportunities and bring them to market without breaking the bank.

Public demand in Australia for genetic testing is already on the rise. The US has established a voluntary genetic testing registry which provides standardised information about tests, their purposes, the likelihood of clinically reliable results and probable actions. Australia too needs a one-stop shop on clinical validity and the utility of genetic testing. Government, medical and nursing organisations need to provide the public as much information as they seek in this rapidly evolving frontier.

It is time to reward citizens to rescue their own health

6 May 2011, *Political Trends magazine* 1st Edition

When we die is mostly up to us. What we eat, smoke and how often we exercise is the strongest influence of our departure date. That should be no business of government, except that dying earlier in life and slowly can cost other people massive amounts of money.

Living a longer healthier life on the other hand is not just a personal good. Additional years of producing and consuming actually repay society's investment in our early years. So the quicker in life we 'hit the health system' the more sustained and aggressive efforts to rescue us become.

Despite a mountain of data and billions spent treating disease, little gets invested keeping people healthier than they choose to be. That's mostly because our personal behaviour is deeply habitual, environmentally dependent and unlikely to change. Interventions like TV public health campaigns are so hard to measure, that we rely instead on GPs for brief interventions and encouragement.

It is hard to imagine that we need more incentive to stay healthy than simply looking and feeling great. The reality is we do. Around 40% of us eat, drink and sloth ourselves to an early and very expensive death. That can be partly due to family background, education, adverse life events and of course, a big scoop of personal choice.

Health maintenance is undermined by discounting and moral hazard. Skipping exercise or hooking into a plate of trans-fats comes at a price; one that is paid far in the future and most likely by someone else's taxes. So we tend to keep doing it. That moral hazard means there is little financial incentive to stay well and even less to use health resources judiciously.

There are ways to combat procrastination, but they are missing in our health system. Healthy choices actually reduce health care utilisation, so we need to pay people to do it. Health-promoting activity deserves reward, and it is deserved in real-time.

The group with most to gain from aggressive health rescue are those with serious risk factors who are yet to develop disease. Since 2002, the Government has paid doctors thousands of extra dollars to offer care plans to these half a million Australians. But it is hard to see how a 'care plan' alone will turn the Titanic towards healthy living. One option is financial incentives for patients to be prudent.

High-risk Australians could benefit from a personal health credit system. Like loyalty programs, 'status credits' reward heath improvements rather than health per se, on a regular basis. Unlike health savings accounts, credits are used to provide near-term incentives rather than fund expensive acute care.

Credits are powerful incentives because they can be redeemed for value at any time. Options might include purchasing health services, covering co-payments or gaps, even promoting ourselves up elective waiting lists. Credits are inheritable and transferable to family, meaning they could cover public childcare, educational costs or other debts to government. Running out of credits isn't punished; it simply forgoes access to additional benefits.

In the United States, insurer United Health Care UHC has implemented workplace-based incentive programs for 81,000 participants across 45 states. Targets are first set based on personal biometry. Credits are then gained for cancer screening and control of weight, blood pressure and cholesterol. Staying nicotine-free also pays, as does good diabetic control. One of the highest cost-drivers is maternity care, so there are extra credits for first trimester sign-up and regular review.

Trying but falling short is never punished. Partial credits are available for alternatives like wellness courses which focus on heart health, asthma, personalised weight management, nutrition, exercise or stress. Like all flat-rate bonuses, they are most compelling to those with lowest incomes. Best of all, credits can be cold hard cash every year. Slogans promoting credits include "Choose to pay less" and "don't leave $900 on the table;" even "take action to get your lowest premiums in 2012."

Personalised health advice through phone and online coaching is far cheaper than tying up hospital-based clinicians. The New South Wales government has embarked on phone coaching for 46,000 patients with chronic disease. US results demonstrate weight reduction and dietary improvement in half of those on phone coaching. Making coaching a fallback for those needing extra credits has increased demand by 500%.

Early evaluation has found 55% earned some incentive and 27% the full amount. 71% achieved their blood lipid LDL targets and 38% their desired weight. Most promising, credits were most attractive to older and lower income workers.

Punishing bad health is deeply unpopular. Taxing fats or sugars is completely impractical. With chronic disease levels rising, a focus on real-time reward offers the greatest potential for behaviour change. Until now, the mantra of "you can't put a price on health" has prevented us paying for outcomes. But in truth we pay for others' bad health choices all the time. So long as my health care is someone else spending, using another's money, it's hard for me to care much about value.

Personalised credits offer me immediate reward for healthy choices. Giving me a financial stake in my health for the first time may be the missing link in stretching our health dollar a little further.

Labor's health and policy reform compromise

21 June 2012, *Online Opinion*

With a federal election just over a year away and the government in the political 'death zone', Labor's health reforms appear increasingly compromised.

Two meltdowns in state health systems emerged last week. Tasmania has hallmarks of being our very own Greece. The minority Labor administration has foregone revenue with extreme Green anti-job policies. No longer able to fund their health system, they have come sniffing to Canberra for a bailout and been rewarded.

Queensland's finances are even more dire according to the Costello Report; at the heart of is Queensland Health, growing at 11% a year. Added to that, Queensland Health is 9% more wasteful than the rest of Australia, including an extraordinary 7,000 people in head office alone.

These revelations show that despite all the magnificent rhetoric, real front line health reform simply hasn't eventuated. Regional cancer centres have been dropped into marginal Labor communities. Millions have been ploughed into super clinics; many are taj mahals in country towns built close to functioning general practices. A perfectly functioning GP after hours arrangement has been completely uprooted, with the replacement call centre simply cost-shifting work into stretched public hospital emergencies.

Australia has three classic tensions in its health system; the state-federal divide, public-private and hospital-community health. Having eight Labor governments in 2008 was an ideal opportunity to address these dysfunctional interfaces but the once-in-a-generation party alignment was passed-up by the Prime Minister.

That leaves this Federal Government clinging to delivering primary health care reform without addressing those three tensions above that undermine it. First, states refused to add their community health services to the mix. Then attacks on doctor groups put much of that sector offside. Former Minister Nicola Roxon's failed attack on the ophthalmologists is case in point. That means the once mighty Labor health and hospital reforms are now restricted to a litter of new and enlarged authorities.

With modern Labor, for every ten bureaucracies they establish or enlarge, an eleventh is thrown in with steak knives. It's simply more sand in the gears and a smaller proportion of service deliverers. It takes quite an effort to invest a quarter of a billion dollars into non-service providing bureaucracy, but the Gillard administration is determined to show it can be done.

Nothing focuses the mind like running out of money and this is where Labor conduct has led. With a predecessor's surplus to spend, the last five years of federal health reform has been a combination of bigger bureaucracies and leaving the real challenges to underfunded but well-meaning Medicare Local staff. It appears virtually every health challenge Kevin Rudd inherited in 2007 will be passed on to Australia's next administration in 2013.

Andrew Laming is the Federal Member for Bowman and Shadow Spokesperson Regional Health and Indigenous Health.

Planning for the end

21 May 2013, *Online Opinion*

We all imagine a life plan, but what about the end of life? It seems remarkable that for such a vital question, we leave it to strangers to decide.

The developed world has exploded with health investment, infrastructure and technology, but our conversations about our final living moments remain perilously unexplored. Palliative Care Australia's *We need to talk about dying* reveals two-thirds of us never discuss this topic with loved ones, and only 15% of people have a plan in place for how we want to be cared for at end of life.

It is daunting and uncomfortable discussion for family members and carers as well. Perhaps that explains why the word 'cancer' is only mentioned 16% of the time by clinicians in their discussions with dying cancer patients.

We all want to keep people healthy and out of hospital. But increasingly, it is appearing feasible to keep the long-term ill comfortable at home. Advance care planners now report they can manage a dying intensive care patient in the home for $2,500 a day, compared to $3,000 to $5,000 in the ward.

Chronic kidney disease and dialysis remains a critical area. Because intensive management can prolong their life, half of them end up in ICU, compared to just a fifth of those with cancer or health disease. At the same time, over half of all kidney doctors feel illequipped to make end-of-life decisions.

Most of us don't realise that a quarter of dialysis patients die each year and a quarter make a conscious decision to cease dialysis before they die. As few as 6% of these patients have an advanced care plan in place. That results in most of these chronic renal patients dying in hospital. Many need not die there and would prefer not to. Reducing burdens on our intensive care beds seems a no-brainer, yet State hospital systems are yet to make the

The great majority of us will reach a point in time where we are forced to choose between a fight for life and the decision to accept death. It will be a time for wisdom, reflection and personal contemplation. As Nobel Prize winner Daniel Kahneman describes it; "slow logical and calculated decision-making."

Our personal values and beliefs are synthesised into goals which inform specific treatment choices. Regardless of our personal views about what follows life, we should aim to travel to that point as comfortably as we can, rather than uncomfortably, surrounded by confusion, over-treatment and dispute between those we love. Health is specifically commissioned to prolong quality life and that should never be replaced by a singular focus upon delaying death.

Governments on both sides and at all levels need to continue to push Australians to developing their own advanced care directives ACDs, particularly those with chronic complex disease. Time spent by clinicians working with patients on ACDs is time, resources and emotional pain saved later on.

It was the General Practitioner co-payment which nearly killed us

3 March 2015, *The Daily Telegraph*

Relegating the Medicare co-payment to history marks Sussan Ley as a decisive federal Health Minister after multiple attempts by Prime Minister Abbott. It started in January 2015 with shredding the failed co-payment schemes of last year. Today she guaranteed the concept won't be coming back any time soon.

There is nothing wrong with a well-designed co-payment for certain Australians to access medicos, but our 2014 versions never came close.

Yesterday's decision to scrap the co-payment can be a turning point for the Abbott government.

It was the most unpopular Budget policy from 2014 and the prime reason for backbencher dissatisfaction. Announcing a co-payment at last year's Budget without any real explanation showed the policy for what it was: all about the money and nothing about quality. Putting the savings into a research fund was a smokescreen that fooled very few.

MPs were not involved in the design of the policy and were unable to sell it to local voters. Those that did were burned, when the original version was replaced with another that was little better.

GP Medicare growth averages about 8% annually. That is mostly due to a flood of new GPs hitting our cities and billing faster just to remain viable. These GP costs are growing slower than hospital costs. Internationally 26 of the 34 richest nations have health budgets growing faster than Australian GP costs.

At the start of 2015, backbenchers wanted 2014 failings addressed but struggled to get heard. It was thanks to the rapid footwork by the Australian Medical Association and the College of General Practitioners in early January that the policy change was achieved.

When Sussan Ley finally acted, she was instructed to undertake "wide-ranging consultation … with doctors and the community … on appropriate Medicare reform." Thankfully, that brief solo flight returned home safely, with no further damage done.

Co-payments had no chance passing Senate, so the bigger question is why that realisation took ten months to take on board.

Now the work of regaining trust in the health area is well under way. Being in government confers no automatic right to barge in and reform Australia's health system. It is a privilege earned through long-term and competent decision-making.

Our two greatest recent health ministers did just that.

Michael Wooldridge in the 1990s rescued private health cover with an exquisite combination of rebates, community rating and lifetime health cover.

Tony Abbott reinvigorated Medicare with bulk-billing incentives and chronic disease management items a decade later. From what nearly every health stakeholder has noted this year, Sussan Ley has every chance of being their equal.

5

economics

Baird's higher Goods and Services Tax plea won't improve health system

22 July 2015, *The Australian*

NSW Premier Mike Baird's plea for a higher GST is a sugar hit unlikely to improve our mostly unreformed and fragmented health system. That is because free hospitals and fee-for-service rewards activity rather than efficiency.

We have private health where the faster one works the richer one gets, next to public hospitals where the faster they work the quicker they go broke. There is no guarantee that extra GST would make any difference to health outcomes because most of healthcare is blind to performance and value. Clever economies worldwide are therefore shifting risk from purchasers to insurers and providers, who are forced to make the tough calls that governments can't.

We have just been through the Rudd years of fiscal expansionism. Few could argue there is much to show for it. Overtaxing and spending arrogantly assumes current problems trump future challenges. Now states are discovering the obvious: switching off spending is exquisitely painful and leads to being voted out.

As John Howard described; going into debt is like taking an elevator down. Paying off debt is like climbing the stairs back out. But he didn't always subscribe to this. As Malcolm Fraser's treasurer he presided over deficits and accumulating debt. Only by defeating Keating and promising better fiscal tightening did the Coalition mantra of budget responsibility germinate.

State premiers innately turn to a federal tax because it is an easier sell. But Mike Baird's 15% GST proposal simply rewards reform procrastination, particularly in the other states which lag behind New South Wales and its record of lowest costs per hospital admission.

The reality is that Australia is a laggard on health restraint. Last decade we were 24th out of 34 developed economies for managing health costs. Among responsible economies with high-quality health systems, we came last. Only the Eastern European economies, Turkey and Chile contained health spending more poorly. Our performance tied us with Greece.

Take Netherlands, which tops the Euro Health Consumer Index. They got there not by spending more money, but with sensible reforms like mandatory health insurance and facilitating patient choice. Private insurers in that case, carry the risks of overinvestment, not the taxpayer. Since 2000, Dutch health expenditure increased less than 1% a year compared to Australia at 1.7%. Under Julia Gillard, growth increased to 2.2% per annum, while the Netherlands bent the cost curve back to an astounding 0.4% in 2011 and Japan actually shrunk health spending.

The most significant practical federal reform has been in pharmaceutical funding. In 2006, I exposed Australia's pharmaceutical suicide gene, which pulled generic drug prices up to a fraction under innovator products. The consecutive price disclosure policies I proposed have been adopted by both sides of politics and will save just under a billion dollars a year.

Premier Baird is right that the public will always want what they can't afford. Right now Australia is big on spending ideas, and meek when it comes to savings. That is why premiers should resist tax hikes; particularly where temporary improvements to budget health will have little impact on population health.

$42 billion spend misses the mark

18 February 2009, *Online Opinion*

Masterpieces reflect their creator. In politics, a $42 billion stimulus package is about as good as it gets. It is a fiscal fantasy where even the wildest dreams can be funded. So to better understand our PM, we should ignore what he says and analyse the design of his stimulus. Not so much its size and timing, which are within the OECD mix, but the constituent parts. It is a stunning narrative on Rudd's view of the world.

First, and above all else, Rudd reveres the intervention of government. Half of his entire package pumps public housing and school construction to offset jobs lost across the rest of the economy. When jobs dry up as most predict, the package's job creation is strongly skewed towards joining construction teams to build public apartment blocks and multipurpose centres or installing insulation.

Rudd funded some economic infrastructure in 2008, but this package's focus on social sector construction makes him an outlier among OECD economies. Just a fraction will be spent on roads, while rail, dams, pipelines, ports, clean energy, science and technology miss out completely. Little provision has been made for the infrastructure which actually earns income for Australia and helps us pay loans back. Rapid deployment of light infrastructure through Councils received crumbs late last year and nothing further in this package.

The flip side of Rudd's faith in government is unease with the role of private enterprise. After all, he blames its greedy extremes for this mess in the first place. He is the only world leader eschewing tax breaks as a recession-busting strategy. Small Business Minister Craig Emerson's offer in Parliament of accelerated depreciation on coffee machines will achieve little in a job-shedding environment.

Rudd's motives for cash handouts over tax breaks isn't entirely clear and he doesn't appear to have learned from experience. December's ABS sales figures showed only 10% of pensioner hand-outs made it into the retail sector; almost entirely on imports from low-end department stores like Kmart and Big W or on household goods. Buying imports helped to avert China's recession but did almost nothing for Australia. The bulk of December's hand-outs appear to have been saved for a rainy day.

As the next recipients of hand-outs, workers and students are even less predisposed to spend than pensioners. Carrying the highest private debts in the world, this cohort is most likely to pay down credit cards and home loans. Such rational behaviour is just what the economy doesn't need during recession. If Mr Rudd had provided these $22 billion cash splashes as a debit card to spend at ten separate businesses, our economy may have received the boost it needed.

The political mantle of economic conservative is a treasured one; earned over time rather than via ad campaigns and potentially eroded by debt, big government and cash hand-outs. All will be forgiven of course, if the Prime Minister's interventions avert a recession, while the Coalition will surge if the economic bad news bleeds long after the cash payments have dried up.

In the end, no one can be everything to everyone. If you are for social infrastructure and bureaucracy, you can't also be committed to small business. The hideous economics of Rudd's $4 billion for home insulation are obvious; a million dollars per job created and $100 per ton of emissions averted.

Let's be frank. Australia had begun to provision for the future, but our modest surpluses and accumulated federal reserves were no match for an economic downturn of this scale. Rudd must run into deficit, but once our surplus and reserves are gone, the only remaining option is to increase Australia's credit limit. That means borrowing, which Australians may brook for vital economic infrastructure, but not so willingly for imprudent hand-outs to astonished recipients who merely pay down their personal debts. Rudd truly faces Howard Gleckman's criticism of "lots of buck, not much bang."

The final observation is that Rudd has overwhelming faith in fiscal measures, rather than working with monetary policy. Unlike flat-lining low-interest rate economies with only quantitative easing at their disposal, the Reserve Bank still has substantial latitude to jump-start private sector confidence. Rudd's fiscal fixation may lead to massive public debts where the same economic outcomes could be achieved with more targeted small business measures as interest rates fall in the months ahead.

The three groaning vulnerabilities in the superstructure of Mr Rudd's package are debts, job losses and the consequent lost perception of economic prudence. They are the squares on the chess board where the Coalition hopes the next election will be decided.

Escaping recession is about rebuilding confidence and re-starting the economy. Australia's policy choices in 2009 will determine the trajectory of that recovery and in turn, future living standards. Every economy will have different recession-breaking strategies. Nations in debt start that race behind; those servicing interest carry weights and those failing to build critical infrastructure to supports business will be speed-limited in the future.

It is fascinating how far Australia's package differs from that of the Obama administration. Australia's package passed Parliament almost unscathed, so it more closely reflects its creator. Rudd's package is timely and larger than OECD comparators, but its constituent parts contain flaws for Coalition exploitation: a faith in government; massive fiscal transfers to States; debt; little for business; and little to protect jobs in vulnerable sectors like mining, retail, services, small business and hospitality. Cash hand-outs will be popular but spending ones' way out of recession is far from proven science. At stake is the Prime Minister's election-winning claim; that of being an "economic conservative".

The Rudd-free account of how we dodged the downturn

1 September 2009, *The Punch*

Australia's momentary brush with recession is over. After less than twelve months we are now leading the world out of what was meant to be the crash of the century.

For a year, we have scratched our heads at the demise of others, cowered from the collapse that never came and frolicked with handouts. Just as we all had our glasses out for another free drink, suddenly it's time to clean up after the party, count the debt and pay it off.

The world's economies move like a cycling pack; uneventful until someone takes a fall.

For centuries, economic and financial crashes have cascaded through nations. Understanding why some economies collapse and others survive is the key to being prepared for the future.

World leaders faced three massive challenges during last September's meltdown; defending their financial systems, protecting jobs and maintaining growth.

It appears Australia has risen to all three challenges. Our post-HIH reforms buttressed our financial system, our government surpluses offered the fiscal space for stimulus to protect jobs; and Australia's food, energy and mineral-based economy supplied the internal demand of the world's fastest growing economies while much of the world's trade stagnated. Other lead economies in contrast were encumbered by ailing financial sectors, heavy debt burdens and a collapse in demand for manufactured goods.

Of these three factors, Australia's export profile is a key reason for our privileged path through the global downturn. Like Norway, India, Indonesia, Greece and Israel, our GDP has been surprisingly resilient. Martin Sommers at the IMF found that the greater the high and medium-tech manufacturing component of a country's GDP, the bigger the GDP fall.

That's great for economies with minimal high-tech manufacturing like Australia, but bad for Europe and the Asian tiger economies. While overseas manufacturers were laying off millions, Australia's commodity sectors were momentarily checked but never looked like faltering.

Starting in 2009, a new trend came into play. Manufacturing nations continued to fall relative to commodity exporters, but banking crisis economies fell even faster, rapidly losing GDP and watching unemployment rise three times faster than those with stable financial systems.

Again, Australia remained out of trouble. Our banks have fee-for-service structures, net interest margins and lending ratios that are the envy of the world, all of which have enabled us to keep well away from the sub-prime and derivatives carnage which took down the powerful peloton of the US, the UK and, later, Germany, Netherlands, Ireland, Japan and Belgium.

The US has pumped three trillion dollars into its banks; Australia on the other hand, virtually nothing. In the end, nations with strong exports and banks lost just a fifth of the GDP compared to those without. On top of that, nations in banking crisis carried twice the government debt into the recession; 67% of GDP against 36%.

Australia's debt-free bottom line and reasonable surpluses meant it could spend its way out of any domestic strife. As a general rule, nations stimulated their economies to the extent to which their balance sheets allowed. Saudi Arabia and China had the reserves to stimulate most, followed by Australia, US, South Korea and Canada. Medium debt economies were next with an average 3% stimulus and finally, high debt nations which stimulated their economy less than 1.6%. When lead economies are taken together, every additional 8% of public debt at the start of the crisis saw an additional percent fall in GDP.

Job losses also tell a fascinating story, particularly when compared to pre-crisis unemployment levels. Though low at 5.8%, Australia's 45% increase in unemployment from 4% is the third largest of the major economies. Nations with reformed labour laws like Australia appear to have shed jobs but preserved GDP, whereas most European economies did the reverse. In a short recession like 2009, job-shedding economies like Australia are likely to prevail because workers are re-employed in growth sectors before their skills become obsolete. Had the recession been longer, job-preservers may have prevailed, thanks to public finances maintaining jobs and confidence through until recovery. Australia's stimulus, stable real estate market and reformed workplace laws all played a role in maintaining business confidence.

As recovery signs strengthen, many commentators agree that a more modest stimulus would have been adequate. Just months after major spending announcements, Australia now has to contemplate pulling up its spending to avoid an interest rate rebound. Australia was the only nation to raise interest rates four times in seven months before the crash, on the pretext of an 'inflation crisis'. Other nations had inflation but kept their nerve.

Because 70% of Australia's residential lending is on variable rates, a 4.25% fall in interest rates was sufficient to sustain housing starts and construction. The $3 billion first-home owner incentives should have been implemented after the interest rate falls took effect. These incentives should also have been restricted to the new housing projects Australia desperately needs, rather than subsidizing profit-taking investors selling off existing apartments into inflated markets.

Analysis of all the world's lead economies tells us why Australia now wears the yellow jersey. Resource exports and our minimal manufacturing exposure held up our GDP. A functional banking sector accounts for much of our 2009 domestic performance. Australia elected to stimulate at three times the IMF's recommendation for no better reason than that it could.

Sure, there was no science around stimulus size and design in 2008, but that was even more reason for a timely and targeted intervention followed by evaluation and refinement. Credit obtained cheaply is cherished least. It is hard enough to resist the temptation to spend away surpluses. It will be far harder switching off the fiscal fire hydrant supporting Australia's charmed economy. We now can't afford to stimulate for a second time in two years. Therein lies the challenge for both sides of federal politics come Budget 2010.

As carnage unfolded last September, world leaders faced three massive challenges; defend their banks, maintain spending and protect jobs. Fortunately, Australia had an answer for each; resilient banks, no debt and a commodity-based economy of energy, metals and food to feed the internal demand of the world's largest economies. In contrast, those reliant on high and medium tech manufacturing collapsed. Australia owes more to its own export profile than any other factor for its privileged path through the global downturn.

Extending the cycling metaphor, Australia's strong banking sector placed it well away from the sub-prime and derivatives melee which embroiled the US, the UK and later, Germany, Netherlands, Ireland, Japan and Belgium. Thankfully for Australia, our big four banks are in the world's top twenty, with fee for service structures, net interest margins and lending ratios the envy of the world. The US has pumped four trillion dollars into its banks, Australia virtually nothing.

Last, Australia had the bottom line to spend its way out of trouble. We know that by looking at other economies. Far from being careful calculation, most nations stimulated as much as their balance sheets allowed. Saudi Arabia and China had the reserves to stimulate most, followed by Australia, US, South Korea and Canada then medium debt economies with an average 3% stimulus and finally high debt nations which stimulated their economy less than 1.6%. When lead economies are taken together, every additional 8% of public debt at the start of the crisis saw an additional percent fall in GDP.

Australia has accrued massive debt through close to the world's largest stimulus package. Some see it as indulgent and wasteful, others as a masterstroke. Too often we look at Australia in isolation, without identifying factors operating worldwide which influence outcomes. Once they have been controlled, we can begin to assess the impact of domestic stimulus packages.

Next, the stimulus payments are seen as saviours. While we can never know the situation without the payments, nor can we attribute better than expected figures to the stimulus. Twenty billion borrowed, ended up somewhere other than our reserves. Maintaining spending isn't that hard when the coffers are overflowing. Australia simply opened the undercarriage and dumped $90 billion into the economy. Twenty billion in stimulus payments was either saved, paid down credit cards and home loans or spent on imports from low-end department stores.

Last and most challenging is protecting jobs. While overseas manufacturers laid off millions, Australia's mostly automated mining sector simply reduced operations and delayed new starts. Combining first home incentives to our existing massive housing underbuild has prevented a price collapse. So long as property construction powered on, there was simply too much activity in the economy for other sectors to fail.

Many with a political axe to grind attribute all this to the stimulus package. Commentators are already thanking the $15 billion schools funding when 97% of it is yet to hit the economy. They laud the $20 billion cash handout. Of all lead economies, only the US tried cash payments, it flopped, and they didn't ever consider repeating it. But with money to burn, Australia did it a second time.

Second, surprise economies like Australia and Norway held their GDP firm while others fell. Other impressive performers include India, Indonesia, Greece and Israel. Martin Sommers at the IMF looked more closely, finding that give or take, for every percentage of high and medium tech manufacture in a country's GDP, economies fell by a percent in the last quarter of 2008. Great for economies with minimal high-tech manufacturing like Australia; bad for Europe and the Asian tiger economies. In fact, Sommer's graph explains GDP changes to within 2% for 22 of the 36 lead economies.

This correlation holds up into the first quarter of 2009, but a new trend appears. Nations with strong banks hold firm while for those in crisis, GDP falls begin to bite. When early 2009 was added to the analysis, the finding still held up, but this time, strong bank economies like Australia performed even better, while banking crisis economies shrunk two and a half times more.

In the first quarter of 2009, banking crisis economies lost jobs three times faster and GDP twice as fast as those without a crisis. Also notable is that banking crisis economies were carrying 67% of GDP in debt, compared to 36% for the rest.

Looking worldwide, it appears some nations have preserved GDP at the expense of jobs, while others have done the reverse. Australia may have the second lowest unemployment in the world but increasing by a half from 4% to 5.8% is worse than most of Europe and third worst of lead economies

More striking is that resource exporters like Canada, Australia and Norway have left the rest of the world behind, losing five times less GDP 0.8% than those without the resources 4.3%, even where their banks are OK.

Australia is indeed top of the class, but examining global trends shows that being a mining economy rather that a manufacturer, having strong banks and low debt pretty much explains Australia's position. No doubt the fiscal stimulus averted some job losses, but Australia's GDP is almost totally accounted for by booming exports.

The greatest minds couldn't pick the crash; our best regulators missed the scammers like Madoff. Australia's Reserve Bank raised interest rates four times in seven months before the crisis at the same time as the US was stimulating its economy in advance of the crash. Among humanity's greatest failings is the fallacy of attribution; two things happen concurrently, and causation is assumed.

After all, it's not about being unaffected, just less affected than everyone else, which is precisely what is destined for Australia.

Doomsayers are doomed to be proven wrong

29 December 2009, *The Punch*

Global economics rarely moves as fast as it has over the last twelve months. Inflation genie, global financial crisis and now, just eight months later, the interest rate rises are back. So was Australia's providential passage through the economic storm the product of great economic management, a fortuitous escape or just an expensive hoax?

Up until now mainstream media have almost exclusively subscribed to the first theory. Slowly some commentators are arriving at the second. Ultimately it is likely to be proven to be the third.

The "never waste a crisis" mentality of politicians means that overreaction is always rewarded.

Those running the models feared underestimating the crash. Policymakers demanded extreme solutions and bureaucrats obliged. According to the prevailing narrative of the time Australia was certain to be swallowed up by last year's meltdown. Treasury modelling demanded a massive stimulus over three years. Virtually everyone received a cheque in the post.

Three months later, the clearly signed Julia Gillard memorial school halls began to appear. Among the mainstream media, economics writers and senior commentators took all the panicked experts at face value.

This time last year Australians were operating a basic assumption that the financial crisis would suck every one of us down the drain and into an unimaginable abyss. Even the Prime Minister got in on the act, describing the GFC as "a truly seismic period where nations move from one epoch to the next."

Back in April this year when the Australian economy bottomed out, I visited five northern hemisphere economies and teased out the three factors which would set Australia's economy apart from the rest of the world. The first was our lack of debt going into the crisis. The second was the resilient state of our banks. The third and perhaps most significant was the close correlation between the proportion of high-tech manufacturing in GDP and the slump in December.

It's these factors which allowed Australia to autopilot its way out of recession but all of it was contingent on hitting the bottom and stabilising.

To better understand where Australia might have gone, we need to examine household consumption of all leading nations in the months after the September crash but before stimuli were deployed. In the four months August through to November 2008, household consumption in Europe and the US was falling at the remarkable rate of over half a percent per month. Even after adjusting for the fact that Australian figures are reported in nominal rather than real terms, the contrast is clear – household consumption in Australia was steady.

Even more remarkable is that the four-month data set is a powerful predictor of the December figures. Across wealthy economies, December household consumption fell around 1% on the previous month.

This pattern is striking across wealthy economies, with the Christmas month dropping twice as fast as previous months with a strong correlation of 0.96. Early stimulators like Germany, Netherlands and Ireland fared better, while Asian nations which don't traditionally celebrate Christmas fared worse. Breaking this pattern in December 2008 were Australia up 4% and the UK up 1.2%.

Of course, these patterns in final household consumption were yet to emerge when Australia embarked on the December cash payments. But Australia's exceptional performance should have been staring Treasury Secretary Ken Henry in the face by mid-February 2009, well in time to moderate the massive commitments made in the following months.

As is often the case, moderation is the best approach. Treasury have belatedly adjusted their GDP forecasts. Just last month, Treasury liquid papered out their 2009 estimates of a 3.6% economic crash, back to a manageable 1.6% hit. That represents around 2% of fiscal deficit which the state never needed to fill. In other words, tens of billions each year we didn't need to spend.

Assuming Treasury is better at calculating past trends than forecasting, we need to ask whether disbursing $100 billion was the right approach. Despite the call for shovel ready projects, only a quarter of school infrastructure projects have been started and interest rates are already going back up.

So how on earth did the 'economic cataclysm' scenario gain such traction? First, we assumed whatever happened overseas would surely strike here. Second, we relied too heavily on modelling. We forgot how limited models are in crisis scenarios because the formulas underpinning them are dominated by data from non-crisis periods. Associations between indicators and outcomes may hold in 99% of cases but completely dissociate in crisis periods.

The other danger for finance ministers was intellectual contagion. With such internationalised economies, big stimulus packages meant greater imports and indirectly 'mutual stimulation. That's why the IMF and G20 told all member nations to stimulate and do it hard, regardless of whether individual nations actually needed it. Just as there are no Porsches for late movers in the stock market, there are no political points for treasurers who exercise caution during a crisis.

However, while reckless bravado might get you a Porsche, it can just as easily lead you to wrap it around a tree while trying to impress your mates. It's one thing to go to the G20 and listen to the horror stories from economies with diabolical banking sectors, huge national debts and no mining revenues. It's another thing entirely to assume we are destined for an identical fate.

What Australia needs is some honest debate. For Labor strategists, suppressing that debate is crucial as it inhibits any inconvenient questions about a smaller stimulus and a smaller debt. That's why retorts like "pulling the rug out from under the economy" and "extra job losses" are the most logical defence to accusations of having panicked and bungled the recession.

Apart from South Korea and the US, Australia's stimulus was the largest in the entire OECD. Why, no one is quite sure. By turning Australia into a mid-level indebted economy like the 'rest of them' the Government may well have forfeited Australia's greatest economic asset.

Between them, Mr Rudd and Treasury have precipitated an over-reaction which will be an anchor on Australia for years to come. Treasury has fessed up and amended its figures. Now its time for Mr Rudd to put national interest over personal pride and take his foot off the stimulus accelerator.

6

education

Reward the good and teach the rest

The Courier Mail, 3 March 2005

After parenting no single career is more vital to Australia's future than teaching. As role models, teachers shape lives and the productivity of our nation. So it defies belief that school teaching lacks financial incentives for their best performers; those proven to achieve results. We can't afford a teaching sector with salary scale so flat that quality graduates choose other professions. Worse still, state governments ignore a skilling skew in teaching, where the highest need schools rely on young and inexperienced graduates.

Financial incentives for teachers based on student improvements against national benchmarks can go a long way towards solving all three of these problems. Far from picking on teachers, this is about knowing what is going on with your children in your school. It is about identifying and rewarding good teachers and providing the drive to excel.

Teachers work within a unionised flat salary scale with their pay locked to experience rather than performance. Professional opportunities have increased for women. Those who once considered teaching are now skimmed into better paying professions, with evidence that aptitude scores for student teachers have declined over a generation. Meanwhile it is society that pays the price; with needy children at tough schools often taught by inexperienced new graduates. It is the lack of incentives that drive top teachers into equivalently paid but less challenging schools or out of the state system altogether.

Likewise, for the sake of our weaker teachers and those they teach, we must intervene before it is too late for struggling pupils. Just as there is unreported medical error, thousands of children today are the unreported victims of poor teaching. The problem is no one knows who is doing what to whom and worse still we haven't even begun to look. Parents, children and teachers alike have right to expect pay to be linked to productivity.

Imagine three teachers. One excels with smart kids; another is skilled with delayed and high-need students, while a third is achieving little progress. They are all paid the same, despite these enormous variations. With performance against national benchmarks unknown, teachers can only self-assess their ability and reflect this uncertainty in vague report cards.

At the state level, we don't know how each education system performs. Before a chorus of defendants cries that no test can possibly measure all, let us look at the national benchmarks to see if there is a problem. Victorian Year 3 students are 20% more likely to fall short of reading benchmarks than their NSW equivalents. Worse, Qld and SA students are an extraordinary 33% more likely to fail. Analysing individual schools and teachers may find similar variation. In health care, such appalling variation would spark outrage.

Brendan Nelson's plan to report to parents in plain English is a start. But parents will be reading junk in plain English if achievements are not linked to national standards. One day, most children will face a cold hard number to earn entry in sought after tertiary courses. So why pretend numbers don't count until it is too late for parents to do anything about it?

The solution is to take the two-yearly national benchmark results a step further. Make it an annual end-of-year assessment. Let parents know annually their child's result against the benchmark. Most important of all, if student scores improve against the benchmark, teachers are rewarded for the value they have added. Under Nelson's initiatives, children having difficulty are identified promptly. Parents gain $700 worth of tutoring vouchers and a clear message that all is not well at school.

Before anyone convinces you that this is unworkable, remember that state education departments already hold test scores from every child, together with their teacher identifier. Beholden to the unions, they are simply too timid to use the information.

Like parents, teachers want to know what works. They need to know how students of different ability levels advance under their care. Consider our three teachers above. The first is strong with talented kids and will seek out schools where his or her skills are epitomised. The second teacher shines with weaker students and will gravitate towards the bonuses available at poor and disadvantaged schools where potential gains are greatest. The poorly performing teacher will be identified early and offered the targeted assistance they need. Nobody loses. Only when skilled and motivated teachers are rewarded for seeking out the challenging areas of their profession, will the current mismatch of teaching skill and student need be addressed.

Denying incentives to our best performing teachers means their talent goes unrecognised. We must encourage the best in our teachers – anything less and our children and their future will pay the price. The trade union stranglehold on teaching and wages is to blame, because they believe students are there for their members, not the other way round. State education departments defend their curricula, resist change and retain the culture that parents should be seen but not heard. Only with information, incentive and intervention, can the quest for improvement begin.

A university avoiding explanations

13 February 2012, *Courier Mail*

Thousands of Australian families cherish the dream of getting their child into medicine. So imagine the dismay when the child of a University of Queensland Vice-Chancellor is admitted without the requisite scores.

Few things are more important to aspirational Australia than the gateway to tertiary education being fair, just and utterly beyond reproach. Especially since UQ receives around a billion dollars a year from government. The idea of alleged high-level fiddling by insiders on million dollar salaries is revolting.

There are two ways into a Queensland University four-year medical program. Top school-leavers are guaranteed entry if they pass a two-year 'provisional' course. Older graduates with high GPA averages are then offered the remaining places. School-leaver entry is years faster, avoids the feared GAMSAT exam and the need for an extra undergraduate degree. Admission is based on overall school performance, an aptitude test, UMAT exam and occasionally vice-chancellerial or excellence scholarships.

Missing out shouldn't be the end of the world. Unsuccessful applicants can reapply after boosting their entry scores, enrol elsewhere or even overseas. Family favours should never be an additional route.

But for someone, missing out did matter. The University suppressed the event for six months and only when it finally leaked, did they investigate and announce mysterious retirements. Only later was the time for new blood' excuse replaced with a veiled confession of events. Ever since, the University has used privacy and privilege to stonewall. All public requests for full disclosure, review of admission practices and even transparent detailing of admission criteria have been refused. Finally this week, the Crime and Misconduct Commission launched a major criminal investigation with a six-member taskforce.

In the minds of many Australian families, that will be a long-overdue advance. Securing an inside lane into the school-leavers' stream displaces a direct-entry graduate two years later. It may also create a public debt of around $100,000 per year to fund extra positions. Medicine virtually guarantees a lifetime earnings around a million dollars higher than most alternatives. That is partly why medicine remains the Holy Grail; entry to which thousands of families save, sacrifice and hope their kids will be accepted.

According to Chancellor John Story, UQ is committed to the highest levels of probity and this episode was an irregularity devoid of misconduct. The University Senate expressed regret but not sorrow. It evokes images of a typing error, or a scene out of Sellers' The Party where someone inadvertently scratches a name on the wrong piece of paper.

But that's not how it happened. A conversation is isolation between two Vice-Chancellors cannot secure a dodgy enrolment. Where was the Dean and School of Medicine in this process? How were irregular admissions funded? What were the second order effects like diverted resources, additional unfunded places or reduced admissions elsewhere?

To be honest, this misunderstanding was just too easy to pull off. Admission to medicine is managed by at least a dozen people and the irregularity must have stood out like a beacon. It is fair to wonder whether fiddling for family members of those in the right places is established practice. Only an inquiry would answer such questions.

In Chancellor Story's words, "by virtue of their positions" the Vice Chancellors accepted ultimate responsibility, so nothing should detract from their "huge and enduring contributions." Apparently the breach is serious enough for retirement at their time of choosing, but not for resignation or further sanction. On such dubious morality, being good enough for a long time is licence for nepotism when convenient. Story's instinct to protect mates demands a closer look at New South Wales university reforms which have replaced Senates with a corporate board structure.

Surely when such a blunder was discovered, it should have been rectified immediately. The student should be required to complete a full degree and get the requisite GPA; the same road taken by her peers without the family connections.

By sitting on this fiasco for months, Chancellor Story must also consider his future. It is not too late to commission an independent audit of entry to the medical faculty over the past ten years and to transparently set out the criteria for university admission. Australians never sought such assurances before because we pay top university brass a million dollars a year to conduct themselves impartially.

Most tragically of all, a combination of familial greed and foolishness has subjected a young student to avoidable humiliation. It isn't too late for the University to be forthcoming and for the healing to commence. It is a shame a major criminal investigation by the Crime and Misconduct Commission is the only mechanism remaining to get to the bottom of this 'forced offer,' the handling of the allegations since and the integrity of university entrance procedures.

Teaching is a profession, but unions try to make it a trade

18 January 2017, *The Age*

Last week, my provocative Facebook question explored teachers, their holidays and whether they really all 'lesson-plan from home'. It was a social media bomb that ripped open the debate about school holidays for teachers that are the envy of many.

Since before chalk and slate was invented, debates around barbecues have probed teacher claims of 'working on holidays', a phenomenon hardly isolated to just one occupation.

So if teachers are performing inordinate and unpaid additional hours, why are we going backwards compared to most school systems worldwide? Is working hard always working smart?

Known as 'click-bait', my deliberately controversial post sought virality and got more than it bargained for. Education unions conducted an orchestra of wailing, petitions and form letters. Much of the online anger stemmed from the fact a politician asked the question. Others felt it was picking on one of the many devoted occupations that performs a vital role for limited remuneration.

Australian schools perform limited external assessment, and teacher support isn't all it could be. More concerning, unions oppose professional development for teachers in working hours without government putting more money on the table.

This month, the 165 largest Queensland high school years 9 to 12 gains were compared for the first time. From the same baseline at year nine, some public high schools triple the number of top score senior students in three years; others tragically diminish that cohort by a third. Despite hardworking teachers everywhere, there appears to be a six-fold variation in public high school performance that has nothing to do with community wealth. In fact, many of the best performing schools are in the poorest suburbs.

None of this information has ever been made public, because school systems prefer to bury indigestible data deep in the *My-school* website. Teachers remain divided across 9,400 campuses nationwide, which makes solidarity more complicated than for instance, nursing unions in major hospitals. This means nurses earn overtime, while teachers carry work home and do it for free. Fessing up that teacher performance actually varies is deemed heretical.

Compare that with nursing. Facing oblivion against higher paid and trained doctors and allied health professionals, nurses fought back and professionalised their degree. They introduced higher salaries for specialisations and a clinical hierarchy that rewarded talent and ambition. Today, nurses and doctors clinically 'self-develop' at home for financial reward. Teachers on the other hand lesson plan at home, for free. Top teacher salaries are only now touching triple figures; something around a quarter of nurses have enjoyed for years.

That is partly due to teachers being confined to salary increments which top-out at a mid-level bureaucrat wage. Unlike nurses and doctors, where the high earners remain on the beat, teachers must abandon the classroom in exchange for further pay rises.

Unions exert significant influence on Labor state education ministers. They oppose Naplan, external testing, publicising detailed school outcomes and as a topper, opposing any rewards for higher performance, to prevent the others being singled out as poorer performers.

Just as in medicine, there should be extra pay for managing the most complex cases. We pay specialist doctors more than High Court judges to manage highest need patients, but deny specialist teachers an additional cent for working with the highest-need students.

It's a weaker nation that curbs this discussion using derision and personal attack. My call is not for an overhaul, but for baby steps towards a system where excellence is formally recognised with more than just a certificate.

If that generates such outrage, it is clear now is the time these entrenched union views be tested, to the benefit of all teachers and our children.

In September 2022 Education Victoria adopted a time in-lieu arrangement for teacher overtime.

This is what I really meant about teachers' pay

4 May 2018, *Sydney Morning Herald*

When a local teacher told me she received a Kit-Kat from the principal as payment for a night of parent-teacher interviews, I'd had a gutful. Like stealing free grapes at the supermarket, we have taken for granted the hours that teachers over and above the 5.5 hours a day they are paid. Teaching is Australia's most poorly paid profession and it's at the heart of why Australian school outcomes are in trouble.

Teacher salaries peak less than nine years after graduation. Their working days are impossibly cluttered. Irrelevant tasks like playground and bus duty are stacked on top of social work and behavioural management, simply to avoid Australia having to pay others to fill those roles.

Teachers haul their unfinished work home, killing their personal lives and wiping out time for postgraduate education that should lead to promotion and pay rises. Long after nursing reformed their promotional and professional structures to survive against medicine and allied health, teaching remains where it was nearly a century ago.

My call to pay teachers for every hour they work was misrepresented by vested interests as an attack on the profession. It wasn't. Much of the magic of teaching lies where it is least expected: quiet counsel under a tree, the excursions that open minds and the extracurricular pursuits. I want teachers paid for these additional hours, including overtime, because what isn't paid is ultimately taken for granted.

However, my key issue is unpaid work from home. It is invisible, it is unmeasured, but the mental health damage is real. When the nation returned to work in early January last year, I had the temerity to ask where all the teachers were. I discovered that they were all at home, planning and not being paid.

Our nation seems to think that overpraising teachers is sufficient compensation for not paying them for their hours of work. Teachers need to recognise that bargaining a few cents here or there in award negotiations will never fix these issues.

First, we must offer teachers the chance to go home like the rest of us and switch off.

Second, the bulk of lesson planning needs to shift out of term time, even if teachers are on-site over school holidays. That is when the pupil-free days should occur.

Third, I want principals to change culture tomorrow and be given a slice of the Gonski resources to fund the extra hours that definitively improve student outcomes.

Fourth, we need an explicit focus on the children that do not gain a year of learning in a calendar year, and not dump the responsibility solely on classroom teachers who are forced to pass the parcel.

Finally, states and territories must replace annual incremental pay rises with a genuine teacher-designed merit-based model rewarding sub-specialisation and further education.

It should include enough time for professional learning communities to engage in formative evaluation. To avoid losing our best teachers, a pay rise after the age of 30 must be possible.

Australia's standards in maths have slipped because other hungrier nations place a higher premium on education.

David Gonski has recognised this and identified best practice but left it to government to negotiate the path. These additional demands about to be placed on teachers for targeted and tailored approaches will need a profession that is revitalised not demoralised.

Only a complete revision of how teachers are paid and promoted will be sufficient. That may fill some with uncertainty and panic, but there are few alternatives at our disposal.

I am relieved that this conversation is now ablaze in every one of Australia's 9,300 school staff rooms, but successfully resolving it relies on this fatigued profession taking a risk and demanding what they deserve. It's clear that Australia is happy to keep sneaking freebies, and saying thank-you.

7
social policy

RU486 – something to be said for considered debate

16 February 2006, *Online Opinion*

Thanks to the Private Member's Bill in Federal Parliament, RU486 is likely to be a medical abortion option for Australian women by year's end. Such approval means additional choices for some, but ironically closes down a chance to debate the ethics of new medications.

The Therapeutic Goods Administration TGA performs the tough job of evaluating safety and efficacy with proficiency and thoroughness. But its mandate explicitly ignores moral and ethical considerations.

Australia has already used Parliament to set the corridors of tolerability for issues like abortion, embryo collection and stem cell research. On the horizon is gene technology, therapeutic cloning, pharmacogenetics and pharmaceuticals in food: each worthy of broad community consultation well beyond the quantitative analysis of whether each are safe and effective. For many, RU486 is more akin to these challenges than it is a mere pill. That is why the community deserves some say via Parliament when major changes to issues like abortion are proposed.

Where substantive community concerns around pharmaceuticals run counter to safety and efficacy, MPs have three options: accept controversial registrations; disallow those registrations with a vote; or write legislation to overrule the TGA every time it happens.

No methodology can hope to satisfy all in such polarised ethical debate. Once the science of safety and effectiveness stacks up, parliamentary scrutiny is probably the closest we can get to having all views heard. After all, it is best to inform community debate using TGA evidence than have uninformed debate in isolation. Worse still is the risk of an unamended Bill – to bypass that consideration completely.

With clear parliamentary support for RU486 in both Houses, a vote on the drug should present no threat to registration. Criticism that politicians can't make the tough calls on philosophy leaves us in an awkward predicament. Democracy must either allow every therapy deemed safe to be sorted out by patients and therapists or hold a referendum.

Currently, the sovereignty of Parliament on pharmaceutical listings is delegated to the Therapeutic Goods Administration. My preference is that where substantial ethical concerns exist, Parliament should retain the option to resume that delegation when required. There is little value in airbrushing concerns away to a scientific panel. Another benefit of parliamentary scrutiny is that community views on termination of pregnancy arrangements change over time. It is disappointing that we view 1970s legislation as immutable and disturbing that we would deny Parliament a philosophical debate on the grounds that we don't share those concerns.

A disallowance instrument is one option to facilitate that debate: a parliamentary mechanism which overturns a decision or regulation. It would only be applied where the safety of specific classes of controversial drugs, deemed safe and effective by the TGA, but where community concern remained. Disallowances must be lodged within 15 days and voted upon within a similar period or it takes immediate effect.

Interestingly, only one Chamber needs to support the disallowance in order to overturn the regulation and block the drug. Currently, RU486 would survive such a disallowance in either House.

That is why it is a fiction to say such parliamentary scrutiny would dissuade applications to the TGA or scuttle RU486 altogether.

Another claim is that disallowance would bury Parliament under an avalanche of applications. In reality, RU486 is the only abortifacient seeking approval. There have been no analogues developed in a decade. Further disallowances could only be moved if new safety or effectiveness issues warranted reapplication unlikely with such an old drug or if a new drug sought to register. That is precisely why we need the option to disallow in the future.

There is a final channel for new drugs through the TGA called the Special Access Scheme. This mechanism provides unlisted drugs for exceptional circumstances like medical research. Such options would not be compromised by having a disallowance option in Parliament.

No solution suits everyone, but there is something to be said for considered debate and the finality of a parliamentary vote that tells me it is as close as we will get to meeting community expectations. Removing such an option burdens a scientific body like the TGA unfairly. As morally challenging therapies blindside the TGA exponentially, the ethical void will become obvious.

This Bill has successfully removed ministerial intervention from drug evaluation. But in the rush to unravel former Senator Harradine's blatantly pro-life legislation, we have lost some vital parliamentary accountability.

Direct debited social solutions

10 May 2006, *Online Opinion*

It is the new battlefront for the Australian welfare system. Imagine Centrelink debiting pensions where parents fail to feed, clothe or educate children. Noting that alcohol, drug use, gambling and violence still ringfence many isolated families from Australia's current prosperity, Families Minister Mal Brough backed direct debiting welfare payments to ensure neglected children were protected, at the 29 April Social Innovation's Dialog.

Catholic Social Services Australia CEO Frank Quinlan found "blaming welfare recipients for their own circumstances" offensive, claiming it "strips them of any remaining dignity in the face of poverty and hardship".

But Brough has his allies. Writing in *Prospect Magazine*, New Labour's John Denham describes the 'Fairness Code;' a set of obligations and opportunities which reward "good" behaviour, contributions and earned rights and punish the "bad". Public services should be for people who are entitled, needy and use them responsibly. Conservative David Willett noted that as lifestyles became more differentiated, it becomes more difficult to legitimise a universal risk-pooling welfare state. People ask, "Why should I pay for them when they are doing things I wouldn't do?"

With child protection an unquestioned priority in Australia, surely direct debit is preferable to confiscation of children by the state in cases where poor life skills contribute to mild neglect. Rather than the welfare lobby's knee-jerk reaction, focus should be upon whether such intervention is morally justified and if so, whether it actually works.

The welfare lobby is wrong to describe the proposal as "a return to coupons and being singled out in supermarket queues".

First, EFTPOS technology means that deductions can occur without stigmatisation. Second, far from being a nanny state, the deductions are merely funding what everyone else pays anyway; utilities, rent and nutrition. The deduction can always be cancelled when the situation improves.

The welfare lobby counters with the need for "comprehensive reform of welfare and marginal tax rates". True, Australia's welfare payments make part-time work less appealing. But the alternatives are worse: lower pensions hurting poor people or slower tapering leading to more middle-class welfare.

The welfare lobby can't have it both ways. An imperfect tax system should not be a smokescreen for inaction on neglected children at family level. Fear of humiliation for those breaching norms must to be balanced with the suffering of their dependents.

ACOSS is even more inconsistent. Lin Hatfield Dodds noted last month that while vulnerable families make correct decisions most of the time, all deserve access to housing, education, health and childcare. But where children are deprived, she rejects case-by-case interview and direct debit as a way to achieve those goals.

While few disagree that denying children food and schooling is repugnant, Brough needs to gain community support by explaining precisely how and when Centrelink would flex its muscle. Neglect can manifest itself materially, emotionally and psychologically. How cases are identified is critical, because direct debiting will impact differently upon people who are mentally ill, those who are addicted or sociopathic, compared to well-meaning recipients who merely lack life-skills.

One concern is that subsuming essential family spending exacerbates matters, if the remaining family budget is aggressively diverted into antisocial practices. All the rent, power and school lunches in the world can't protect children from appalling home situations.

Additionally, Centrelink intervention will unfairly single out welfare recipients, leaving workers exempt. Beveridge, the father of British welfare, would have countered that the middle class only pays for the welfare state if they share in its benefits. That includes minimising the social cost of malnutrition, child neglect, youth disengagement and unlawful behaviour.

Brough is right that untied welfare can present dysfunctional families with the means for their own destruction. But only randomised and controlled research in the Australian setting can clarify whether welfare debiting is the next big thing or an exercise in futility.

What is for sure is that after the first round of a comprehensive community debate, the welfare lobby has been a little too slick in their dismissal of Brough's proposals. Should the Cape York Institute and other Indigenous-led interventions report encouraging results, the welfare lobby must then decide whether it will support expanded trials. Even more controversially, could such strategies be viable across mainstream Australia, which so often differs only in its ability to conceal familial dysfunction.

Laming established and Chaired the Australian Parliament's Friends of Early Education from 2011 to 2022.

Burqa ban is an overreaction to extremism

1 October 2014, *Daily Telegraph*

We are the world's most multicultural nation. Part of that package is to welcome the burqa together with every other garment.

Sure we need to be able to identify citizens at security points or when accessing taxpayer-funded goods or services. That applies equally to those wearing balaclavas, helmets and masks.

Simply identifying someone in that circumstance shouldn't be cause for offence. If that person insists on dealing with a female, they should also be happy to wait until a female security officer is available to deal with them.

In the private sector, it may also be legitimate to identify people in banks, collecting items of value and at certain times in law firms and health clinics.

But, if there isn't a vital reason to identify someone, then we shouldn't be refusing to serve people simply because we can't see their face.

Like wearing a robe, a cross or a shawl, it is a conspicuous form of religious expression, but it needn't have any impact on the rest of us.

Senator Cory Bernardi may want burqas lifted at the doors of Parliament House but, once people are identified, leave them alone.

We may not be able to see faces on subsequent security footage, but nor could we if an offender placed a handkerchief over their face.

If there isn't a vital reason to identify someone, then we shouldn't be refusing to serve people simply because we can't see their face

It is remarkable that France, Belgium and the Netherlands banned the burqa. It really reflects how they lost control of their borders and are now reactive. Spain is reconsidering a burqa ban after overturning it last year, while the UK has stood firm on freedom of dress.

In the current climate, extremists can only recruit supporters if the mainstream create the conditions for it, starting with mistreating the peace-loving mainstream Muslim population.

Taking a crack at the burqa or halal certification are all examples of temptations best left alone. On the other side of the equation, it is reasonable to expect more from Muslim leaders than statements of abhorrence or distancing themselves from extremism.

We need them taking the lead in every corner of their communities to identify radicalism and fringe groups early, before leaving the rest to our law-enforcement officials.

Issues such as the burqa generate news and animate a few. But, compared to child protection, youth unemployment and social isolation, it is a non-issue. That is why, in the current environment, we should pause to contemplate the nation we have built and where we want to take it.

Telling people how to wear their clothes shouldn't rate a mention.

Same-sex marriage postal vote does the Coalition's political fortunes no harm

9 August 2017, *Sydney Morning Herald*

This week's Coalition party room meeting on same-sex marriage was as close to a basketball swoosh as you get. A three-pointer that barely touched the rim, the mood was positive and as close to unanimous as the Liberal Party gets.

A plebiscite was the Coalition 2016 election promise and we now know after a month of hysteria, the government is full court press on a people's say in 2017.

The issue of same-sex marriage is emotive, which explains why last month's Newspoll found the nation split, with 45% in favour of a plebiscite, compared with 39% for a Parliamentary vote. The Coalition is the only party whose membership and politicians reflect the polarisation of the nation – hardly a party "out of touch".

As of Monday night, same sex marriage proponents now understand that killing off a legislated plebiscite in the Senate simply replaces it with a postal alternative. It is the nightmare scenario for marriage equality proponents, but does the Coalition's political fortunes no harm whatsoever.

Much of the centre of the Australian electorate supports marriage equality in phone polls, but it is far from clear if these people would bother to vote in a postal plebiscite. Recent polls may be robust statistically, but they are junk politically, because a voluntary vote requiring completing and submitting a form could filter out a third of voters. It increases the chances of a "no" vote because the young who lean towards yes on phone polls are least likely to vote.

The Coalition realises that while distracting, this debate isn't politically damaging for us. It played little role in the 2016 national election result because the two extremes of marriage policy have already joined the major parties and election campaigns.

Unfortunately, the focus on methods has prevented a clear picture of what would follow a postal plebiscite. A 50% plus one national "no" vote closes the book for this election term. But the Coalition will revisit its position prior to the election in 2019, which may include a conscience vote. This would mean both parties going to the 2019 election with effectively the same policy, further neutralising this issue at the next election.

In contrast a "yes" vote in the plebiscite triggers a conscience vote in Parliament. Forget whether it is binding or not because, unlike Labor, the Coalition mandate a position on conscience issues. The handful of MPs pushing for marriage equality will be free to vote as they choose, meaning the law will change. I for one will vote according to the will of my electorate; which means I may defy a national "yes" result if it is "no" locally – not that it would impact the final result.

This is a plebiscite that doesn't require public funding for each side. In fact, a case can be made for a media advertising blackout, to prevent the avalanche of international financing that has contaminated overseas marriage votes. Most of us just want to have our say and move on.

A plebiscite will be an energising moment. We are not Bill Shorten's infantile nation that can't handle the debate. That attitude would have killed off the historic Indigenous Australian referendum in 1967. But get ready for a surprise result, because the outcome is far from clear. My advice for the warring parties is to campaign hard, clean and don't demean.

Laming ran SSM plebiscites as part of community surveys since 2010, and pledged to vote according to the community verdict.

Pill testing will do more damage than it prevents

19 October 2017, *Sydney Morning Herald*

The recent push for pill-testing in response to music festival over-doses will do more damage than it prevents. The ACT Labor government endorsed pill-testing for November's *Spilt Milk* music festival. The somewhat Orwellian Safety Testing Advisory Service was offered at the Festivals and Events consortium as a free service to attendees.

This group emanates from Harm Reduction Australia HRA, and includes the Australian Drug Observatory, Noffs Foundation, DanceWize and Students for Sensible Drug Policy.

Thankfully this ill-thought solo-flight was cancelled when it became apparent that the venue was federal land and the appropriate permissions would not be forthcoming.

But so-called drug experts won't let the slip slow them up, so when the next music festival flirts with the same idea, it is vital that the hard questions are asked in advance. Until now, colorimetry was the mobile test of choice, but as Police have reported, the error rate was significant, with all tests requiring expensive confirmation.

The *Split Milk* proposal went a step further, with Infrared spectroscopy, which applies differing light absorption to precisely identify if a pill is pure or includes anything from ratsac to detergent, or even a dangerous hallucinogenic like 25C-NBOMe; known to have caused several deaths in Australia in the past twelve months.

However, spectroscopy has limitations, with a recent Harm Reduction Journal article noting 'interference is very common and causes difficulty in identification.' It is hardly a ringing endorsement for a service that waves through illicit drugs as being okay for consumption.

David Caldicott, a Canberra-based emergency medicine specialist has been a defender of the technology, saying it is 'tried and tested' worldwide but provides no evidence it works.

The ACT pill testing website may be more reliable, stating "the available literature does not provide evidence that pill testing prevents deaths among festival patrons." This leaves high performance liquid chromatography as the gold standard, but this option destroys the sample which defeats the point for consumers who hand over their hard-earned pills.

The general argument for pill-testing runs as follows: drugs are everywhere; abuse inevitable, so every pill tested is one less that may kill. The leap to a fancy spectrometer inside a tent is seductive, but presents a new set of risks,

Safework Laboratory's Andrew Leibie says on-site technology is inadequate; it will not detect some drugs at all, occasionally misidentify others, and most concerning is missing low levels of potentially lethal contaminants.

Ironic that music festival signage prohibits illicit drugs but seem disinterested that they are awash with them. Patrons carry drugs in with minimal checks, then a testing tent provides the cover organisers need to appear engaged in the issue. It is certainly cheaper than footing the bill for emergency overdoses which are lumbered on the taxpayer.

Pill testing fails to remove pills from circulation. Festivalgoers have wide discretion regarding what to do with pills. Regardless of test result. In the pressure of the moment, forfeiting a fifty-dollar pill isn't easy at the best of times, let alone surrounded by revellers and without cash to purchase alternatives. The obvious risks include on-selling to other patrons as pills that have being 'tested and cleared,' or pursuing and violently confronting suppliers at the festival is also a risk.

An even more diabolical outcome is cocktailing, where a dirty tablet is crushed and mixed with many clean ones in a game of reverse Russian roulette, in order to dilute the toxic effect across sufficient users that no one is harmed.

Finally, pills deemed safe or pure are potentially taken in larger quantities and more often. Clean does not equate to safe, because 100% pure MDMA kills users every year. In the UK where pill-testing has been widely trialled, deaths from new psychoactive substances has continued to rise.

This entire cascade of stupidity exposes why it is simply more sensible to replace pill-testing with drug detection systems. If pills must be tested, let it occur in a non-intoxicated state, away from private events and where appropriate supports and counselling is available.

Illicit drugs are called that for a reason. A quick field test doesn't make them ok. Pill testing serves the needs of dealers and suppliers at the expense of a whole new set of complicated and potentially dangerous outcomes consumers. That is why this entire pill-testing boondoggle should be ditched.

Agony of the ecstasy pushers

25 July 2019, *The Australian*

Music festival pill-testers continue to skirt the truth in their campaign to expand their services beyond Canberra.

At last weekend's *Splendour in the Grass* music festival at Byron Bay in northern NSW, the equipment was again on show, with claims that lives are saved with testing.

Only Hobart City Council has signed up so far, earning a strong rebuke from federal Health Minister Greg Hunt during Tuesday's question time.

Testing is about identifying deadly contaminants, but the inconvenient truth out of the NSW coronial inquest into the series of drug deaths at music festivals is all deaths were due to an ecstasy MDMA overdose combined with environmental factors such as the weather, hydration and other drugs.

But it gets worse. Under sustained questioning last weekend, Canberra emergency physician and testing proponent David Caldicott continued to muddy the waters, claiming that upgrading to more advanced gas chromatography GCMS would allow more accurate measuring of the dosage.

It fell to toxicologists to mop up with the details, explaining that GCMS determine dose only with additional testing and infrastructure – in other words, transporting expensive mobile laboratories to every music festival in the country. To determine an actual MDMA dose, the entire pill needs to be sacrificed for testing, defeating the point of the test for users who want their expensive pill back. Only suppliers with batches to sell would benefit.

Previous festival testing relied on mobile infra-red technology called FTIR. This reveals nothing more than a series of graphical spikes, which are correlated with known substances. It rarely detects more than three constituents, or anything new, or something that is less than around 10% of the sample. Worst of all, most homemade pills have patchy ingredients, meaning scraping different surfaces can yield completely varied results.

Despite this, Caldicott's passion receives mostly sympathetic media coverage and is rarely subjected to interrogation. His claim that pill testing saves lives is now parroted by a range of harm minimisation supporters, many of whom, like Caldicott, support the legalisation of MDMA.

A useful metaphor is the dangerous thrill of BASE jumping, which clearly is not condoned but likely to happen regardless. Nonetheless, the government is hardly going to place parachute inspecting services on skyscrapers.

Caldicott's strongest argument appears to be that testing is used overseas. However Australia's festival temperatures can be double Amsterdam's, presenting serious risks of hyperthermia and dehydration not seen in Europe. Combining even small MDMA doses with caffeine, alcohol and other drugs here can be lethal. Many consume pills before arriving at events to avoid the sniffer dogs, meaning that many attending pill-testing facilities are already too intoxicated to counsel.

In addition, the ACT trial had no age check to prevent minors being counselled or police checks to prevent suppliers sending in samples of their inventory for assessment.

The decision to discard pills is left to the user, which opens up possibilities such as on-selling, cocktailing with other drugs in an attempt to dilute the danger or, worse, retribution against festival dealers who supply about a third of the material. These hypotheticals need to be understood with simple behavioural research in the field before testing is condoned by groups that should know better, such as the Australian Medical Association and the Royal Australian College of General Practitioners.

It is only a matter of time before a tested pill is implicated in an overdose death. Potentially that person won't be the individual who signed the personal indemnity form in the tent. It is a $1 million lawsuit just waiting to happen, with costs borne by the taxpayer and presumably the event organiser.

Policing simply collapses when it is forced to step aside for "harm minimisation". Soft-touch policing at ACT's *Groovin' the Moo* festival charged just one adult out of 20,000 with possession. In contrast, *Splendour* in New South Wales was twice the size, with more than 200 were arrested when police were allowed to do their job. In the ACT, less than 1% of festivalgoers elected to test pills, raising a potential selection bias issue where only those least likely to overdose actually engage the service, mostly out of curiosity.

Testing proponents need to address these concerns instead of airbrushing them away as they did on stage at the *Splendour* festival forum. Entering the space between illicit consumers and their euphoric weekend needs at a minimum, criminal checks, age checks, drug swabs, gold-standard testing, user-pays, follow-up checks, plus an onsite intensive care unit and helicopter transport out of the red zone. All of this is anathema for the pill testers and consumers, as it is for taxpayers expected to foot the bill.

State governments, oppositions and police services remain lukewarm on festival pill-testing not because they are dinosaurs but because genuine concerns arise when the state enters an illicit market, offering low-quality information from entry-level technology. Passionate tent people preaching restraint is welcome, but giving revellers half the story from a fancy machine risks more lives than it saves.

Laming took the battle against pill testing to music festival debates including Byron Bay's Splendour in the Grass. The policy is yet to be adopted by any state government.

No one can be safe until we tackle drugs scourge

30 January 2021, *The Australian*

Last week, city elites far from central Australia were horrified when I raised petrol sniffing in remote Australia as more important than dabbling with our national day.

Within hours, substance abuse became real in my own neighbourhood, when a few corners from my Brisbane bayside home, amphetamines in a 17-year-old running a red light visited evil upon an innocent community.

We mourn three beautiful souls this week because experts in the justice system couldn't provide the protections we needed.

Never was it clearer that from the city to central Australia, there is no safe refuge from substance abuse. For all the talk on the street about tougher sentences, however, it is depenalisation that offers more hope. But that requires commonwealth reforms to provide teeth to the rehabilitation journey.

Australia's welfare system pays cash to youth, and plenty of it. The 2019 EDRS Ecstasy and Related Drugs Reporting System Drug Trends in NSW tells us that users are likely to be renting, smoking crystal, and finding it easy to obtain. Most have some work or study, but more than half are receiving commonwealth payments without conditions.

Two addicts cohabiting with dependants receive more than $1,300 a fortnight to fund their habit. And while Covid has impeded the import of precursors and increased prices, those out of work are about $19,150 better off, thanks to the Covid payments.

After rent, those sums afford a 0.25g hit twice a day each per fortnight, until the next Centrelink cash transfer arrives.

Sadly, magistrates have little understanding of these economics, with youth revolving through courthouses, back to the ATM, then resorting to crime as their addiction grows. The judiciary can't even use the results of an amphetamine test to determine if addicts are safe to release.

Commonwealth reforms to stem welfare spend on drugs have been drafted, but lie dormant in the Senate, opposed by Labor, the Greens and some independent senators concerned about human rights. What they should be concerned about is the early and firm intervention for ice addiction.

Appearing in Court for certain violent offences, or failing to meet Centrelink obligations, should trigger a precautionary hair bulb test to detect ice use in the past three months. A positive test then precipitates regular mouth swabs to identify recent use, together with wraparound care, starting with welfare paid onto a cashless debit card. Centrelink would then help with managing income, ensuring there is food and nappies for any dependent children.

With welfare not paid in cash, maintaining a drug habit is near impossible. Dealers and suppliers lose interest; they don't want to be paid with bartered food or phone cards. Even if someone turns to theft, addicts are frequently caught, allowing the cascade of support to start before the cascade of car stealing.

While there is no magic bullet with Ice addiction, current law enforcement is like a torn parachute. That is why confronting addiction early and switching off the money is the only thing that activates an honest conversation with users about their detox journey; something that rarely happens when the next hit is as close as the ATM.

Under reformed laws, co-operative work by state and federal agencies would be provided to magistrates. Attending residential detox could then be part of a community order, and welfare would be restarted only after consecutive drug tests were negative, and compliance at longer-term non-residential rehabilitation had been established.

Most of Australia's youth justice legislation was crafted before we understood how violent Ice users can be. We need to stop blaming the professional case managers and give them, and the police, the laws that offer hope of a solution. These laws don't apply to pensioners or the disabled, nor would drug testing be done randomly. But once an offender is known to be addicted, we need to stop the revolving door that puts innocent lives at risk.

Matty Field, Kate Leadbetter and their unborn child had a right to a beautiful life. If that means fewer choices for addicted individuals using taxpayer funds to buy methamphetamines, then Australians will call for that in every city, town and parliament, when sittings resume next month.

8

Aboriginal Australia

Indigenous problems fester in too-hard basket
7 May 2011, *The Daily Telegraph*

In remote Australia, our country and its leaders have created the world's most dysfunctional patch of humanity.

It's a place rolling in welfare money, but with little to buy and less to do. John Howard conquered many challenges but in his final year as prime minister realised, like all before him, that indigenous policy proved too hard. His emergency intervention managed to shake the status quo, swapping nutrition for intoxication at the price of consultation.

Tragically, Labor have left the intervention in suspended animation, too scared to repeal it and lacking the wit to improve it. Labor's way is that everyone gets welfare and in return does nothing if they feel like it. There is no mutual responsibility to feed and protect children or get them to school. Prime Minister Julia Gillard's latest offering is more of the same.

Labor consistently avoids offending their urban Aboriginal elite. Rivers of money have not stopped the rivers of grog, but that is our punishment for invasion, rather than poverty evasion. No wonder nothing changes.

Borrowing from the Coalition's "tough love" approach, the PM announced this week that when their kids reach six months of age, teen parents must return to work, training or study or risk having payments suspended.

Fumbling as it is, Australians will welcome a bit of spine. But on closer look, remote Australia is exempted.

In remote Australia, where childcare centres are rare, middle ear disease makes Aboriginal kids deaf in noisy classrooms. Instead of smaller learning groups sitting under trees, we rig classrooms up with bigger loudspeakers.

Local language has disappeared. Labor ripped that out years ago, thinking that poor school outcomes were due to kids speaking more than one language when in fact it was due to a host of complex social issues.

No wonder school attendance rates are less than half in some areas. Schools need to be made both attractive and relevant to these Aboriginal kids.

Making schools less relevant guarantees more truancy, vandalism, petrol sniffing and crime. Kids get a criminal resume faster than an academic one. Making schools less relevant places impossible burdens on parents already struggling with the challenges of surviving in remote communities. Removing incentives to learn removes the chance to be capable and to provide for those you love.

Working adults and school-attending children are non-negotiable components of a civil society. It is the only path by which a dwelling becomes a home, a cupboard fills with food and Aboriginal children get a chance for lasting improvements in their lives.

Andrew Laming is the Opposition spokesman for Aboriginal health and regional health services

More talk, no action in Indigenous affairs

30 June 2011, *Online Opinion*

The world doesn't need another Opposition Indigenous spokesperson bagging out the Government about Aboriginal health. But Jenny Macklin celebrating yet another round of consultation plumbs new lows in Labor's anthropological approach to central Australia; watching, measuring and talking about gaps, but little more.

Macklin has released so many reports on Indigenous affairs, she doesn't know if she is Arthur or Martha. A visit to her website shows an entire page of links under her watch; links to reports done by wildly committed but now mostly forgotten authors, all noting the lack of data or that things are much the same as the last report.

Last week, they ran out of new titles for new reports. Last Friday's *Stronger Futures in the NT* had a familiar ring to it. Two years, a month and a day prior, Jenny released virtually the same thing in *Future Directions for the NT Emergency Response*. Both committed to exactly the same thing; more listening. Like the apology for the past, Labor loves documents titled 'Future' because the present is fast becoming an era of indecision, weakness and waste.

Then like now, Jenny used the same headshot photo. Only the adjectives have changed. Back then Aboriginal people were feeling "hurt betrayed and less worthy" than other Australians. In 2011, it has been dutifully updated to "anger fear and distrust." Interesting that adjectives change at all, because Labor hasn't done much except watch the Intervention like a soufflé through the oven window.

In 2009 Jenny was "consulting throughout the NT, wanting to hear the views of those affected by the measures." After two years of spectating she is now "talking with Aboriginal people ... so we can build stronger futures together."

Reading much further would be pointless, so let's try to define what a stronger future really looks like under Labor. In housing, only around half of the $1.8 billion can be accounted for in dwellings. The rest appears to have been skimmed by spivs, charging up to ten times the value of the refurbishments delivered. It now emerges that it cost $1.7 million dollars for every single Aboriginal job created; even if most just swept slabs, carried materials and kept out of the way.

True, school attendance bounced up from 40% to 60% when the Coalition implemented the Intervention. But under Jenny it has flat-lined at 60% ever since. Labor haven't the wit to apply existing laws on school attendance or to financially compel dead-beat parents to drop their kids off. Isn't that part of getting a parenting payment? Pearson achieves over 80% attendance using Jenny's funding, but she hasn't found a way to implement his ideas because her mates privately hate Noel.

Hyperendemic unemployment was once due to lack of jobs. But now that there are more unskilled mining jobs than there are working-age remote Aboriginals, that's no longer an excuse. Truth is Labor took an axe to mutual obligation in 2008. Their new 'hardship clause' exempts anyone with less than $5,000 of liquidity from being breached. The entire cohort of Aboriginal youth can now refuse interviews, training or job offers with impunity.

The unavoidable price of sparing communities was alcohol-seeking migration to regional towns. Alcohol damage so often correlates with unemployment. Australia is relatively unique in its creation of a welfare world were boredom and alcohol tear communities to pieces. Only when we get kids to school and transition communities back into work, will alcohol again be safe in these communities.

Taken together, the Labor fixation with rights despite all the lovely talk about 'stepping up' and 'getting tough' prevents it enforcing laws which apply to everyone else. They perpetuate the double standard which Pearson is trying to remove; the fact that if you are in a remote Aboriginal community, you are exempted from rules like sending kids to school, taking up a suitable job or training, paying market rent, repairing wilful damage, or alcohol laws. That runs contrary to most of human civilisation where subtle elements of compulsion play a limited but important role.

It is true some interventions are unpopular, none more so than the ones which work. Labor credibility is stretched to the limit in Central Australia. Before election 2007 they snuck around communities talking about how they would axe the ghastly intervention while to the rest of us they talked tough to be like John Howard.

Upon election, Kevin Rudd fell over himself to apologise for the actions of his predecessors. But truth is his legacy is just as appalling, worse when the wasted goodwill and dollars are factored in. I have little doubt someone in the future will have to apologise again to Aboriginal Australia for the inaction and report writing of the last five years. All kids must go to school, welfare must be conditional upon accepting suitable work, grog consumption has its limits and kids must be protected. All we need is a government prepared to enforce the rules that exist across the rest of the country.

Aboriginal kids a no-go zone for health census

13 September 2011, *Online Opinion*

As a young top-end medical researcher in the 1990s, my mentor taught me that presented with information in an appropriate way; Aboriginal Australians were perfectly capable of making their own decisions. In 2011 we appear to be forgetting those lessons as fast as we learn them.

Next year's National Health Survey will randomly interview 50,000 Australians and offer a sub-sample of those interviewed the option to provide blood and urine samples. Every Australian that is, except Aboriginal children who make up almost 40% of Australia's Indigenous population. In a glaring throw-back to the era of the Aboriginal Protector, special advisory groups have decided that all Indigenous kids are to be excluded. Apparently they can handle the survey questions like the rest of us, but not the provision of blood and urine samples. These experts have removed the rights enjoyed by every other Australian; to contribute through the provision of samples to an accurate picture of Australia's state of health.

That sounds pretty racist to me. Consulting on how to do things is appropriate, but I won't stand for national institutions like the Australian Bureau of Statistics being told by expert panels that Aboriginal children are off limits. Sure we can look at different ways to do things, but a 'black ban' is something that we should have consigned to ancient history.

These five expert groups making this determination include the National Indigenous Health Equality Council, the National Aboriginal and Torres Strait Islander Health Officials Network and the National Advisory Group on Aboriginal and Torres Strait Islander Health Information and Data. None of them are household names. I doubt if any of their members have ever lived in the squalor of central Australia or know just how critical it is to gain an accurate snapshot of blood profiles, nutrition levels and renal function. For the rest of the world, the inclusion of sampling in a national health survey is gold standard. In Australia, that opportunity is being denied to the cohort with most to gain.

The people who really matter in this debate are the Aboriginal children whose long term health outcomes are at risk, their parents who have been denied the opportunity to have their children included in the survey and also the Australian taxpayer who is forking out billions trying to close the gap in Indigenous disadvantage.

It is telling that when contacted directly, a number of these committees indicated that they never advised anyone that blood and urine testing was 'culturally inappropriate' for indigenous children. That is significant because 'culturally inappropriate' was the precise grounds advanced by Minister Snowden's office this month to justify the exclusion.

Aboriginal parents have been consenting to blood and urine tests by doctors, nurses and research ethics committees for decades. So it is hard to see why it is suddenly so culturally inappropriate that kids must be excluded. Sure some parents might refuse, but plenty more will participate. It is up to the Australian Bureau of Statistics to ensure the sample is adequately stratified and representative. The results are too valuable to pass up.

Such a position has wedged the ABS, which is now compelled to assure us that this exclusion won't lead to an information gap on Indigenous children's health. How curious, because the same ABS remains determined to include indigenous children in the 2017 Survey. So testing kids later this decade is vital, but a baseline while we are investing billions to 'close the gap' isn't.

The people who really matter in this debate are the Aboriginal children whose futures rely on evidence-based social policy. In contrast, it is the Government's gain if bad news goes missing. There is no surer way to ensure that happens than never collect data in the first place.

Right now, Australia appears so paralysed by panels, paperwork and paternalism, that it will be another six years before Aboriginal parents enjoy mainstream decision-making privileges. Worse, it may be even longer before taxpayers learn about the true state of Indigenous children's health. Minister Roxon can undo this mess with a single telephone call to the ABS, but that call won't happen if government fears what such a study may uncover.

Laming completed the assessment of azithromycin in paediatric trachoma, out of Darwin's Menzies School of Health Research. It is now standard treatment.

9

politics

To stop the refugee boats, start by setting up a visa queue in Quetta

10 January 2011, *The Australian*

Twenty years ago, Gul Rasul lost his leg above the knee while clearing Afghan villages of landmines. He was helping families repatriate from Pakistan, but his price paid was living a nightmare: hours of agony in the back of my ambulance and a lifetime living with a severe disability.

This story is important because a man from a small, persecuted Shia minority found a way to rebuild his country. He re-joined a local demining operation that same year with a prosthetic limb and his younger brother replaced him in the field. At any time he could have rolled the dice with people-smugglers and taken a decent shot at Australia, but he is one of the deserving thousands who elected to stay and rebuild.

Regional instability is a given across the Middle East and parts of south Asia. But it is being aggravated by the 1951 Refugee Convention, which drives people into neighbouring states to apply for asylum, only to discover massive waiting lists and years of delay. It is eminently safer, faster and more efficient for the UN to process refugees when they first cross borders; it also restricts criminal trafficking mostly to non-refugees.

Two-thirds of Australia's arrivals originate from Afghanistan and Iraq, nations with democratically elected governments that we helped establish. Half of these arrivals are escaping little more than poverty and pockets of instability.

Because the laws of refoulement don't apply to these non-refugees, they should be immediately returned to UNHCR safe zones in their region for economic reintegration. That doesn't occur because we have a federal government offering each of them the option to appeal Immigration's determination to a review tribunal, and a recent High Court determination allowing them to appeal that appeal. Even then, we merely invite them to return home.

The Australian-funded AliceGhan residential complex in Kabul is an ideal resettlement base. It can accommodate 6000 people but is mostly empty. Only when non-refugees are respectfully returned home can they warn others of smuggling's futility.

The further from source we determine asylum, the harder and more costly it is to resolve. The most tragic option is what we do now: label it a complex problem, watch boats limp over the horizon, then process applicants onshore.

In office, Labor has made more than a dozen policy retreats and is reaping what it sowed, with more than 6,000 people arriving annually. The first hint of progress was the government's leak last month that Afghanistan might finally accept the return of failed asylum-seekers, which was a regular occurrence under John Howard. Coalition immigration spokesman Scott Morrison pointed this out, arguing the need to address the problem at its source. Supporting refugees in their countries of first asylum is more effective than dealing with those who ultimately make it to our shores. He is right to demand a fresh look at how we implement and interpret the Refugee Convention in the 21st century.

Displaced and persecuted families such as Gul Rasul's may engage smugglers as the only alternative to long UNHCR resettlement waiting lists. Once in Pakistan, roadblocks around Quetta prevent Afghan asylum-seekers from reaching Western authorities in Islamabad to lodge a direct application. It's wrong that wealthy nations sign up to a refugee treaty, only to make success geographically improbable.

Expanding cross-border processing would mean thousands more applications, but a consistent bar for refugee status would mean the quick dismissal of frivolous applications. Our goal must remain identifying true persecution as expediently as possible.

Wealthy nations are more likely to accept UNHCR resettlement requests out of Pakistan than they are from Australian detention centres. That's why it is in our interest to better resource border processing, then engage other target nations to shoulder the resettlement load, particularly those not pulling their weight in securing or reconstructing Afghanistan.

Malaysia's visa exemptions for certain Muslim states is the segue for smuggling by air into Southeast Asia. Next, Indonesian boat crews operate as drug mules of the trade, with little to fear from our courts. Ten-year jail terms followed by non-voluntary extradition to the feared Kerobokan prison would end these journeys. But the federal government can't even finalise an Indonesian prisoner-exchange agreement. Footing the incarceration costs of its complicit citizens is one way to induce Indonesia to stop boat trafficking before it starts.

Immigration loopholes at home add to the attraction of smuggling. The chance for family reunion visas lures extended families in Afghanistan to pool resources, smuggle individuals on to boats, then hope the remainder can follow. Until every person deserving asylum can get it, we should limit reunions to spouses and minors of the persecuted.

Australia is obliged to defend its sea borders, but surveillance and processing along our northern shore is expensive and the risks we impose on our service personnel often unnecessary. A fraction of the billions this government spends running detention centres for non-refugees would fund facilitated return for thousands of families into the new Afghanistan and Iraq.

Regional instability, and the people it displaces, is a fact of life;

commercial people-smuggling shouldn't be. Australia must strengthen cross-border processing in Pakistan, return non-refugees to their region for UNHCR appeals, provide real deterrence for Indonesian smuggling crews, and reform our family reunion program. Only with innovation at source rather than desperation along our north can we secure our maritime borders and help those who need it most.

Andrew Laming is a Coalition federal MP from Queensland, a former landmine clearing medic in northern Afghanistan, and a World Bank consultant.

Assange no hero, but deserves better

15 December 2011

If you break the law overseas, don't expect government to bail you out. Julian Assange hasn't been charged under any laws for Wikileaks and that makes Julia Gillard's abandonment of an Australian citizen so disappointing.

The Wikileaks founder is a divisive figure; evoking reactions of admiration, loathing, love and horror for releasing a mountain of classified US cables. But whether he is a control freak, a socialite, arrogant or whatever, he deserves to be treated fairly. No matter how much you hate the release of cables, it doesn't make it illegal.

Like most major media outlets, Wikileaks operated an anonymous drop-box for information and US marine Bradley Manning filled it in spectacular fashion. Through a possible plea bargain, the US appear intent on establishing that far from voluntarily offering up the cables, Manning was coerced to do so by Assange. That case seems even more implausible following this week's revelations that Manning googled Assange and Wikileaks over a hundred times on his work computer beforehand.

Sure every nation must have its secrets, but secrecy shouldn't be overused. One place not to place state secrets is in cables which can be accessed by around a quarter of a million public servants. It is simply too easy for a 19-year-old to download them onto Lady Gaga CDs and carry them home.

Further along the information supply-chain, it is difficult to assign any more blame upon Assange than *The Guardian* or *New York Times* which disseminated the content with delight. It now appears Assange offered the opportunity to redact highly sensitive material out of the cables, but the US refused. If that offer to filter out sensitive material was passed up, it suggests there wasn't much in the cables to sweat about. US officials now concede that no assets were moved or redeployed in Afghanistan as a result of Wikileaks. Passing up the offer to redact and the reality that it has been business as usual since, makes it hard to maintain the argument that Wikileaks was a mas-sive haemorrhage of state secrets which risked compromising the free western world.

That's probably because diplomatic cables are little more than the everyday truthful and uncluttered observations of foreign ser-vice hopefuls. This mostly banal and anodyne content is occasionally spiked with acutely embarrassing content about powerful people. So its little wonder few of them will now stand up for Assange. It is also vogue for politicians to be pro-national security. That means judging first and not being bothered to ask questions on the way through. Julia Gillard is the exemplar. Having assumed Assange had broken 'some' Australian law, she even canvassed cancelling his Australian passport, effectively making Assange Australia's first political refu-gee. With such initial hostility, the Prime Minister can't even do her job on behalf of this citizen without looking like a back-flipping hyp-ocrite. Little wonder she has been mute ever since; a far cry from her approach to David Hicks.

Sweden's legal system is curious in places and unfamiliar to most of us. They are entitled to seek Assange's extradition and the minute he lands, either place him into incommunicado detention or tempo-rarily surrender him to the US by 'mutual agreement.' That's a mutual agreement which doesn't involve Australia.

Meanwhile in the US, a grand jury continues in secret session in the notoriously pro-national security state of Virginia. Even after over a year, there is no indication if charges can or will be laid. But given high-profile US politicians have called him a terrorist, an en-emy combatant and sought his extrajudicial killing, one wonders if a fair trial is possible, or any protections exist under the first amend-ment.

The attacks on Wikileaks include subpoenas on twitter accounts and a complete financial embargo, including shutting down all forms of financial services and payments. That has effectively starved As-sange of the funds required to run his defence. We are reaching a point where things are done to Assange for no other reason than they can be dreamt up by those who are mildly annoyed.

The evolving plan to bump Assange along legal systems to get him in front of a US grand jury is disappointing. If the US believes an Australian citizen has a case to answer, at least be upfront about it. If Assange has done anything more than offend the powerful few, it is time for that case to be fully elaborated and heard by a truly independent judiciary.

10

environment

Carbon coupons may be the way to go

7 July 2008, *Online Opinion*

Australia must relinquish the dream of targets, timetables, caps and trades until China, India and the US are on board. A nationally based carbon coupon system is a promising alternative.

Forget 2010; Australia needs to admit that the giant developing economies are not getting any closer to embracing a target for greenhouse gas emissions. With the world's financial markets at tipping point and Australia's economy still heavily reliant on coal, a premature "cap and trade" system would be foolhardy.

A far more sensible route is to move now to a national carbon coupon or hybrid system without the auctions, caps and international trading. As we have seen with water, enormous savings are possible with the right incentives for business and households.

Released last week by Reserve Bank of Australia board member and ANU Professor, Warwick McKibbin, *"Building on Kyoto: Towards a Realistic Global Climate Agreement"* outlines just such a domestic scheme. A national plan retains sovereign control and delivers what business seeks; the economy-wide capacity to manage risk to promote deeper investment in carbon mitigation.

Setting targets for the year 2050 may be politically seductive, but India and China can't even predict their own growth ten years out and they're certainly not about to curtail it. We know from negotiating free-trade agreements that "mutual action" is more likely to succeed than complex global "cap and trade" arrangements, where actions of recalcitrant states simply shifts the burden to others.

McKibbin proposes national carbon emission coupons; essentially emission permits of varying durations which obviate the need for an auction or direct taxes. Coupons can't be traded internationally but additional annual coupons are available from the government at an international price. Coupons are divided equally; half to our energy intensive producers according to their 2001-5 average; the other half distributed per capita to all Australians. Expiring permits create a downward sloping carbon curve over many decades. Just as shares pay dividends, Australian citizens can rent their coupons back to industry as compensation for increased costs of living associated with higher energy prices. The higher the costs, the more the coupons are worth.

A known carbon curve means more certainty for energy providers and users, allowing them to make long-term technology investments where a fluctuating carbon price would not. Each nation avoids hitting its diminishing carbon curve, when its industries become more efficient or acquire coupons from less efficient rivals.

Hedging against carbon risks makes sense to a liberalised finance sector. Growth industries can hedge by acquiring coupons or gamble that technical improvements induced by carbon constraints will keep them affordable into the future. The arrangement is preferable to collecting carbon taxes up-front then attempting to compensate the vulnerable through imperfect redistribution.

McKibbin's proposal retains decision-making within sovereign states, with the safety valve option of industry purchasing short-term permits from the government at an international price. So there is an international component, but one state's irresponsibility doesn't flow through to others.

Distributing coupons to the population means we each have a stake in the integrity of our national system, rather than a central-

ised "cap and trade" arrangement where every participant from individual to nation has an incentive to dishonestly understate their
consumption. A coupon-holding population has good reason to self-
regulate and prevent abuse.

Australia was a black sheep of the international community on
Kyoto, taking the principled but unpopular position that it was impossible to set realistic targets. Nations made little attempt to meet
their Kyoto targets, no one took the penalties seriously and too
many nations were grandstand spectators. Australia's celebrated
ratification came after the agreement was already in disarray.

Rushing into an emissions trading scheme by 2010 has serious
implications for Australia. No other country has such a tiny global
footprint 1.5% of global greenhouse emissions yet as much at stake
economically from a flawed "cap and trade" system.

Unfortunately for Australia, our reliance on hand-picked but
non expert economists is leading us down a very different post-
Kyoto path. As if making up for lost time, we are racing to design
a technically perfect carbon tax which faces evisceration by exemptions demanded by politicians. That could do more harm than
good.

Many nations will struggle to sign up to a carbon tax for which
the costs are large and uncertain. The impact on machinery and vehicle sectors, chemicals, metals, paper, plastics, agriculture and food
will vary for each signatory. International carbon trading means external shocks are transmitted to other nations in a "zero-sum game".
Lastly, signatory nations have to churn carbon tax revenue back to
compensate vulnerable citizens. This is a very impure science at the
best of times.

Climate change's rate-limiting steps are the giant developing
economies. This week, China supported the election of Robert
Mugabe at the UN. When one also considers China's actions in
Darfur, it is clear that self-interest still trumps altruism. For the
other half of the world with incomes below $10 per day, there will

be little appetite for adding a 20 cent carbon tax to fuel which is already subsidised.

Last century, 44 nations tried to fix the price of money to a gold standard at Bretton-Woods. They failed. Enforcing a global price for carbon will be even tougher. Elements of McKibbin's proposal avoid the pitfalls of a global "cap and trade" and deserve urgent consideration. Unlike the gold standard, this time we don't have the luxury of decades to urge imperfect administrations to adopt a perfect carbon tax.

Garrett green loan fiasco

24 May 2010

Garrett's bungled Green loans disaster is a slow motion replay of the home insulation bungle argues Andrew Laming.

It all seemed so legitimate when announced before the 2007 election. Fifteen hundred experts accredited by the Australian Building Sustainability Association would deliver 360,000 home assessments as a precursor to thousands of interest-free green loans.

But by early 2009, the Rudd-inspired fiscal panic meant departments had to spray money into the economy like never before. The first blunder was by a DEWHA divisional head who ignored mid-year warnings from assessors and deregulated assessor training numbers. August 2009 warnings from the ABSA direct to DEHWA were also ignored. The promised 1,500 assessors became 11,000 in just six months. In the guideline vacuum, training organisations short-cut four day training into two, with the unfortunately named Lucky Strike Traders blacklisted by ABSA for training up to 40 assessors at a time.

Because each home must receive DEHWA authorisation before an assessor can enter, the assessor glut and ensuing contagion led to a daily peak of 96,000 DEHWA hotline calls and up to 22,000 assessments. Assessors left family members on hold for entire working days and the promised online booking system never eventuated.

What were meant to be two-hour home assessments became shorter and shorter. Householders reported ill-trained assessors breezing through in 15 minutes, omitting mention of photovoltaic solar panels or solar hot water, then waiting weeks for their promised report.

An early beneficiary of Garrett's mismanagement was the private firm Fieldforce, which carved out a cosy 6,000 assessments per week deal with DEWHA without having to negotiate the call centre. So when the DEHWA call centre choked, many sole operators turned on Fieldforce with accusations of special deals. In reality, the Fieldforce innovative call centre system showed that in any policy challenge, private sector innovation trumps a government department every time. Fieldforce had 7% of the nation's assessors but snatched 30% of the work. That's only because the rest of the program was held hostage to DEWHA incompetence. Ironically, Fieldforce has now offered to run DEHWA's call centre to show them how it should be done.

When Garrett's 2009 Christmas gift to assessors was half an hour's notice that the hotline would close until January 11, everyone except Fieldforce lost their livelihood. When the program finally re-started, it collapsed again under the weight of the four-fold oversupply of assessors. Suddenly, Minister Garrett was all about saving his own job and nothing about greenhouse abatement or the jobs of those who trusted him.

In suspending the program last week, Garrett wiped out the only good reason for performing assessments; the green loans. That's because he promised 200,000 loans but only achieved 1,500 at a hideous program cost of $60,000 per loan. In fact only one in 300 homes assessed actually obtained a loan. Banks like Westpac refused green loan applications due to 'significant delays … verifying assessments with government."

Garrett needed a political solution. First, he used the undisbursed green loan money to buy off 5,000 assessors with the offer of 42 weeks work; just enough to get him past the next election. But the national limit of 15,000 assessments per week means just three per person or six hours work a week. For the 85% of workers who are full-time professionals, it's the equivalent of being fired. It's barely a living wage after tax and expenses.

Second, Garrett cut the other 6,000 assessors loose. They have invested around $20 million already; a 4-day $1500 course, $660 for ABSA accreditation and the $1000 for insurance. It's all Garrett-inflicted loss. Of the $10 million paid in compulsory insurance premiums, no claim has never been made. With assessors unable to even touch the dwellings they visit, its hard to understand why indemnity could not have been part of the government's standard public service cover.

Incompetence must reach levels never previously witnessed to collapse a three-year program in just nine months. Choose from insensitivity or incompetence to explain the false hope for assessors, the glut of accreditation, the $20 million out-of-pocket, the exorbitant ABSA registration, the $10 million in unnecessary insurance and ultimately the 6,000 Australians tossed on the scrap heap. All the lipstick in the world can't save this pig of a program.

Unions abandon their members on carbon

26 May 2011, *The Punch*

In search of mates for their unloved climate tax, Labor phoned a friend and the ACTU answered on *The Punch* last week. That was predictable. But it was the shallowness of Ged Kearney's contribution which surprised many, because it demonstrated a limited understanding of the debate and scant regard for the best interests of her members.

The ACTU case is simple enough; it is the same as Labor's. Belief in the climate science and that someone must pay. The ACTU's more nuanced perspective is that their members shouldn't pay a cent. In the pantheon of climate hypocrisy, that places Kearney right up there next to Paul Howes. Someone must pay; so long as that someone isn't me.

Credit to Kearney for conceding she isn't an expert in the field. Nor am I. But ignorance is no excuse for refusing to seek simple answers to fair questions on behalf of her members. It is implausible that an ACTU president could be both unaware of membership doubts around both the science and the tax. It is breathtaking that she is unwilling to address them with reasoned reflection.

While the ACTU is correct that someone must pay, it's the 'when and how we pay' which really matters. These complex questions have engaged the minds of protagonists globally, but not the ACTU.

Their disengagement on questions of national interest is a concern; questions like when and how to pay, the need for international agreements which reduce protectionism and the role of future technology in abatement. Surely unions care about avoiding carbon leakage and the export of union jobs. They need to urgently establish which of their members benefit and how many may be harmed by a carbon tax so they can play a role in that transition. At the moment, all they appear to want is a free ride.

With such climate conviction, it's an extraordinary double twist with pike to then demand complete immunity from a carbon tax.

Focused on destroying their sworn enemies, it's all about the 'big polluting companies' who should not be 'let off the hook.' That tired dichotomy of nasty corporations crushing toiling honest workers resonated in soviet Russia, but that old class warfare mentality isn't valid anymore.

The ACTU ignores tax incidence by denying taxes on energy generation pass invariably to consumers. Of course, the carbon tax will hit union jobs and hip-pockets along the supply chain. The question runs beyond job and income protection. Unions should be asking how variably fuel-stressed union families will be fairly compensated over the medium and long term. Equally, unions should be monitoring whether multinational entities shift effort and reduce domestic hiring as they seek higher returns offshore.

There is also a bigger picture. Unlike taxing carbon at consumption, current taxes apply Pigouvian principles to hit production. That hurts economies like Australia because we are forced to self-tax our resources which are overwhelmingly exported. Blue collar and middle income earners have the most to lose with this approach, but it is a fact lost on the ACTU. Supporting a tax on production which trickles unpredictably down upon its membership suggests they are more a front for the Government than an advocate for their members.

Finally, the ACTU appears seduced by the 'finite resources' argument; that our ore, coal and gas might run out if we don't have a carbon tax next year. All three are likely to take us into the next century. We didn't need Mr Rudd's plan by November 2009 and despite residual hysteria, we don't need a clumsy carbon tax while around 90% of the world's commodity exporters are doing nothing. Just like global trade arrangements, climate negotiation will take years and possibly decades to achieve. Forcing up fuel prices at the bowser for Australians in 2012 is political masochism which achieves little.

Australians generally agree that market-based solutions are the most effective. Rudd's, Gillard's and Abbott's all qualify. The question is who needs to be dragged into that market to achieve desired carbon reductions. Economists may prefer the miniscule theoretical benefits of Gillard's uber-tax but 90% of it is avoidable churn and the administrative costs are enormous. That is why Abbott's direct and verifiable purchase of abatement is so attractive. Funded through existing consolidated revenue mechanisms and waste reduction, abatement is guaranteed while ordinary consumers with inelastic consumption are protected.

The ACTU can't be expected to support Abbott's plans, but their members deserve an honest appraisal. Gillard's approach risks disproportionately hurting low-income earners who are more reliant on essentials and across a range of fuel-stressed arrangements, impossible to precisely compensate. The ACTU also conveniently ignores the massive waste cuts which the Coalition has promised. Kearney should be more nuanced on these issues rather than refusing to take Abbott's plan seriously.

Climate debate here and globally is really a battle of economic redistribution. It's about how much rich people pay to poor and rich nations pay to poor. Redistribution is precisely what tore the Copenhagen negotiations apart. Rudd survived as long as he did by keeping debate focused on the morality of protecting the planet. For Gillard, it's really just a rich tax where the proceeds are used to buy the support of her voter base through vague promises of compensation.

By global standards, the average ACTU member is among the world's wealthiest 12%. There are 2 billion worldwide living on less than a couple of dollars a day who will never afford a seven cent per litre fuel tax. That is why the ACTU needs to explain why union jobs and income should be protected in a globally workable scheme.

Agency theory describes aligning the actions of those who represent us with our own. ACTU members pay to have their interests represented. Instead of being ideological puppets for ailing Labor governments, unions should be doing all they can to get the best possible carbon solution for the country, not just blanket exemptions for their members.

No guilt, no shame in rejecting this tax, Australia

3 August 2011, *The Punch*

Apologies in advance to those with fixed views on a carbon tax. It is time the majority of Australians had a say. Well over half of us have shifted from supporting carbon pricing leading into Copenhagen to now opposing. In early 2008, my seat of Bowman had the highest carbon trading scepticism of seats polled by the Climate Institute; at 16%. It now runs at nearly 70% and it helps to remember why.

Let's deal with the shame issue up front. Most Australians have little interest in national shame, be it border policies, the apology, shame about our live exports or the fact we mine and smelt.

Most Aussies are tired of being told by the elite we should be ashamed of our per capita emissions. We don't leave our vehicles on in the garage at night. Our emissions correlate perfectly with our wealth, our energy intense export profile and that with the world's second lowest population density; we travel further. I see no shame in that

We are sceptical of the European Union and their rules on everything. They have weird trade protection quotas, which undo the great work their foreign aid provides. We are unmoved by their guilt trips on how we manage our borders, because the jury is still out on their approach. No shame there either.

We are in the lead pack of nations on renewable energy, neither out in front nor lagging. I don't want to fall in a hole like Spanish solar, nor have a €75 billion feed-in tariff like Germany which delays the onset of global warming by nine hours.

Our massive trade competitors like Russia, Brazil, South Africa, Mexico and Chile may be poorer, but we don't want them taking our commodity jobs and investments in the name of 'a climate solution'. Massive miners like the US and Canada are actually walking away from action.

No US presidential candidate will take a carbon tax to the 2012 election. The UK is ultimately part of the EU and much like them, so we understand them joining in. But in our part of the world, the vast majority of south-east Asia watches us tax ourselves for the inputs they value add and export worldwide. The emissions according to the EU are ours.

The world reaches agreements not by going it alone, but through coalitions and confidence-building. We don't sign landmine treaties on day one; we get everyone on the page and sign together. In fact, once you sign up, much of our diplomatic suasion is surrendered.

It's the same with trade negotiations. Nothing was achieved by simply dropping trade barriers and feeling good about ourselves. It is a painstaking and detailed process and Australia should depart from that approach with caution.

With 16 new or increased taxes from this Government, why can't the 17th, the climate tax, be in place of an existing one Norway replaced part of its payroll tax and called it a carbon tax to reduce the cost of living burden. Why should we give our PM nine billion dollars a year to hand around as she sees fit, when much of the last $110 billion was spent so poorly during the crisis? Surely I don't need to list the programs.

There is not even a whiff of a carbon tax among our top three trading partners or among any of our commodity competitors. Outside the EU, nations like Singapore, Korea and New Zealand are hardly likely to move in on our share of export markets. Being brutal, Australia's carbon tax announcement has led to no new nations contemplating one. So the momentum argument lacks just that.

China is busy selling the world cheap solar panels and replacing old dirty coal-fired power stations at the end of their life with new ones. But that isn't emission trading. Even India's a dollar a tonne on carbon is economically negligible. Far from inspiring others to join us, going it alone generates hundreds of commercial asymmetries which our competitors will rationally perpetuate by not acting.

The other great irony is that Australia's 'compassionate left' appear unmoved by possible job losses at home. Back in 2007, they railed that "not a single worker be worse off under certain extreme laws". Suddenly losing an industry or two, reducing growth, viability or new jobs barely rates consideration. Union bosses will always back a bad Labor Government over any Coalition alternative, so they happily abandon their own members and support the tax.

Last, there is the NBN argument, that we are wealthier if we transform our economy early. But solar power still costs 42cKwH, well above the residential tariffs we pay of 28cKwH and 6cKwH for coal. It is equally the case that others do the heavy and expensive lifting and Australia capitalise on new technology when it is cost-effective.

"There will be no carbon tax under the Government I lead" will be Gillard's political obituary. Some jest that Bob Brown leads, others wonder if it was naked deceit, or just a post-election strategy to appear to be a 'conviction politician' Gillard's best excuse for the deception has been that she never foresaw a hung Parliament. So name the crossbencher who gave Gillard an ultimatum of "deliver on a carbon tax or I join Tony Abbott?" The answer is no one.

After an impressive career in Opposition, too few days in the Lodge and facing a resurgent Tony Abbott, Gillard simply panicked on that pre-election Wednesday. That's OK.

But given the choice between a promise to 22 million people and a pet policy, she chose the latter. That's why an overwhelming majority of middle Australia remain sympathetic to the climate issue but want nothing to do with the PM's new tax.

11

international affairs

Bougainville's long wait for autonomy

24 May 2005

Voting is routine in Australia, that we find it hard to imagine waiting a generation for a chance at autonomous elections. After thirty years and a dozen federal elections in Australia, the tiny Pacific island of Bougainville finally gets its chance this week; to elect an autonomous government of its own.

My family moved from Brisbane to Bougainville in 1970. Aged four, I vividly remember massive plantations, secluded beaches, abundant seafood and tropical fruit. We never realised when we departed, that the friends we left behind would grow up in a very different Bougainville, one where civil strife would displace a third of the population and cost 15,000 lives.

The daunting job of monitoring the election process rests with eleven members of a United Nations coordinated international observer team, drawn from the Commonwealth, the Pacific Islands Forum, Japan, New Zealand and Australia. Following 190 mobile polling teams means criss-crossing 12,000 square kilometres of jungle-covered islands, unsealed roads and the odd volcano. Some villages are reached only by walking tracks, while others are on remote atolls hundreds of miles out in the South Pacific.

The elections may take up to a week, with a result expected in the first days of June. The only thing familiar to Australians about the Bougainville vote would be the ballot boxes. For a start, it all happens outside under the trees, cordoned off from onlookers by nothing more than twine and bamboo. Village polling teams comprising local public servants work all day without so much as a betel nut break. A row of loyal scrutineers sit transfixed, tallying voters and best-guessing their intentions. It is hard to imagine a more transparent process.

Unarmed police are conspicuous, but thankfully their role has been limited to supporting polling staff and shooing away the dogs. Indelible ink marks those as they collect ballot papers. That's four ballot papers to be precise; one for President, one for their local member and one each for their regional women's and ex-combatant representatives. Even in remote villages where lower literacy leads to longer queues, entire communities wait patiently. For those who miss out at busy booths, the only alternative is to truck, trek or boat to nearby villages on following days.

After such a long wait, it is not surprising that Bougainville set an ambitious timeline to elections. That started with approval of its new constitution by Papua New Guinea's parliament late last year. Since then, the island has stuck doggedly to its ambitious election timeline, even where that meant a six-week campaign, just a hand-ful of rallies and many voters knowing little of their local candidates.

Our most remote stops were the villages of Telatu and Sapani. From the vehicle track, they were nothing more than wisps of smoke through foliage. In the first village, only a handful had voted by day's end. In the other, we met polling team 17 who proudly displayed completed count sheets. Most had already voted by early afternoon including 70-year-old local chief Paul Salu. Wizened with a walk-ing stick and clutching home grown tobacco rolled in newspaper, he proudly proclaimed in tok pisin to all gathered, "I was aged eight or nine during the war. I brought food to Japanese soldiers and met a Commander. After the war I tried to learn English but never got there. I live up in the mountains now; my family looks after me sometimes. Now I have walked down three miles to vote and I am about to walk back up there again,' he says, gesturing upwards into the mist.

A coastal village in Selau was my team's final polling visit. After voting closed, ballot boxes were sealed to a round of applause from onlookers. The chief then walked us down to a breathtaking beach to show us his three crowded volleyball courts.

"I built these for the younger ones so they don't turn to jungle juice," he explained. "One day we want to brew our own beer here for export. If we can get some money together, then we can build proper houses for our families and afford education."

As an honoured guest, my hands and feet were washed of evil spirits in the traditional way. Reminded that as the visitor, I should reciprocate with a gift of food, I realized that chocolate biscuits aside, I was running on empty.

Sensing my hesitation, our host stepped forward. "I guess you aren't travelling with a spare pig are you? How about a sack of rice; we do hotel pick-ups." Autonomy in Bougainville has surely found a friend in entrepreneurialism.

These contrasting stories in neighbouring villages are likely to be replicated across the island this week. The challenge for Bougainville's new Assembly will be to weave together a common future from a painful and often divided past. Whether through providence, local commitment or the dividends of strong regional partnerships, opportunities must be seized when they come along. Bougainville senses that this week is one of those moments. That is why this election is not so much about party platforms and ideologies as local communities stepping forward, person at a time to have their say, be dabbed with indelible ink and hold that hand up for all to see.

Andrew Laming is the government representative to the UNESCO National Commission

Remember our fallen

2 February 2010

Australia's armed forces have a century of distinguished service in every corner of the globe. Each individual soldier's part of that proud history is most tangibly represented by the medals they were awarded. For the members, they are a badge of honour and a token of gratitude. For the rest of us they are the physical evidence of that person's service and sacrifice.

For that reason it is surprising that Australia has no mechanism to recognise those who make the ultimate sacrifice or are wounded or injured in service. While Australia currently awards campaign medals for active service and medals of valour for acts of selfless bravery, at present there is no distinct recognition for those who in serving, sacrificed their life, their health or their ability to continue their active service through injury.

The closer medals come to retelling an individualised story of service without undue complexity, the better the system works. Unfortunately medals can't tell the full story, if they only recognise being in a location for a minimum duration. Under our current medal system an individual receives the same recognition regardless of whether they were killed in action or simply spent 30 days in a particular location.

The other challenge is eligibility due to the potentially ambiguous distinction between injury and wounding. Defined criteria will always be tough on some as they form a qualifying floor, below which is nothing and just fractionally above which is the complete award. This will be hard on some wherever the line is set, but it isn't grounds for not recognising anyone at all.

There are a range of international precedents for this proposal with the United States, United Kingdom and Canada all awarding a specific medal for service personnel killed in service. Instituted in 1947, New Zealand has the Memorial Cross for the next-of-kin of those killed on active service, including peacetime operations.

Two medals can be awarded for mother and wife. Canada has the Silver Cross, initiated in 1919. Importantly, Canada and New Zealand award these as civilian medals and don't recognise wounding or injury in service, unlike the US. Service personnel wounded in action are awarded the Purple Heart. Families fly service flags from homes, businesses, churches and schools. The flag displays a blue star for each serving relative and a gold star for any killed in action.

Some like Redland's Ted Harris have proposed the reintroduction of an Australian Memorial Cross; nicknamed a Mothers' Medal. There is precedent. From WWI, the Mothers' Widow badge was issued to those who lost a family member, with a star for each relative lost. A similar medal with stars was presented to the nearest female relative of those lost in WWII. In the end the mothers' medal lost its cache with coupons posted in the mail, allowing next of kin to collect medals from the post office.

Being a civilian medal, the killed in action KIA medal is awarded directly to the next of kin. Just as in Canada and New Zealand, a civilian medal would not clutter the military medal order of where scheme and it could be worn by families at times of their choosing rather than be a matter of military protocol. A medal represents more substantial and palpable recognition for families than a clasp, which can be worn by those wounded or injured even when they return home.

The final proposition is to strike a comparable award to the next of kin of Australians giving their life in peace-keeping or non-military service. Eligibility would be any service eligible for consideration for the Humanitarian Overseas Service Medal. For the 800 Australian families who have lost a loved one in either military or humanitarian work, such recognition is long overdue.

Australia and the Philippines

10 October 2012

It is Australia's invisible northern neighbour. Philippines is south-east Asia's first democracy and only Christian nation. Most of us know at least one of the 230,000 Pinoys who live here in Australia but that is about it. Virtually none of us learn their national language of Tagalog, trade is negligible and tourism effectively non-existent.

This week, Philippines hit our headlines for all the right reasons. After forty years of civil war in the south, popular new President Noynoy Aquino struck a peace deal with separatist Muslim group MILF. The previous day, he had released details of a national audit of his predecessor President Arroyo's regime, which found $3.2 billion dollars had vanished in corrupt payments. Apparently 744 officials will face possible prosecution.

But the veneer of good news is little more than skin deep. Aquino has devoted half his first term to fighting Arroyo appointments like the Chief Justice. Last week he had Arroyo herself re-arrested, foiled only by her dash to hospital for medical care. It all makes for great TV, but fabulously little impact on the ground in this feudal and impoverished nation of over a hundred million peace-loving people on seven thousand islands.

Last week candidacy lists for the 2013 election were submitted to the national election commission. Because political parties are weak to non-existent, incumbents jumped on the 'Liberal Party' bandwagon under Aquino's banner to ensure they retained access to federal funding largesse. Such politicians are known as butter-flies, seeking out whatever light is brightest at the time. In a nation where opposition is truly the place not to be, using incumbency to align with the President is the latest game in town.

Philippines is actually cursed by its high political participation levels which exceed 80% at presidential elections, because it confers legitimacy on a system in which only TV stars and famous families win. Every Philippine Senator is a millionaire. Term limits are bypassed by shuffling or rotating family members through Congress, the Senate and mayoral positions. For all the frustration that should evoke, everyday Filipinos appear mostly indifferent, save for a peoples' revolution every couple of decades.

Nearly 10% of Filipinos work overseas, with their remittances contributing a similar amount to the national GNP. Tax collections are 13% of GDP which is half what it should be. Of that amount, it is estimated a third goes in corruption. A quarter of the population earn less than $1.50 a day. The lucky ones earn $4 a day harvesting rice. Workplace productivity has flat-lined now for a decade. Walk into many retail stores and you can hardly get to the shelves there are so many staff on the floor.

Xstrata's massive $6 billion Tampakan copper and gold reserve could add 3% to Philippine GDP. Currently, the entire project is held to ransom by local municipal administrations which have banned open-cut mining in defiance of the national government. Welcome to the home of sovereign risk.

Transparency International lists corruption in Philippines at 134th worldwide with only 45 nations below it. That is because being a whistle blower can be a death wish. If not you, then it is your family who is rubbed out. The lucky ones are given 72 hours to leave the country. 32 journalists have been assassinated since 1992 in this nation where scribes are too often issued a gloc pistol before a voice recorder.

In the overwhelmed judicial system, wealthy families can buy off witnesses, judicial officials and avoid prosecution, even in the appalling case where civilians and journalists were buried alive in a trench with a backhoe. Ironically the only way the corrupt are caught is when they stumble on someone wealthier. Like the customs official driving his Porsche in a road rage incident, who opened fire on a family member of his own commissioner.

The solution in a nation where trust and transparency are scarce commodities isn't simple. One option is a plethora of public private partnerships where user pays, and the government promises to stay away. That works for a roads, rail or bridges with a revenue model but is less convincing for social services like hospitals and schools.

Filipinos need a place to report corruption, but sharing a death wish with an underpaid civil servant hardly seems worth it. Aquino has embarked on a massive push to publish on-line all procurement and issue local municipalities with certificates of 'good housekeeping.

Australia is making a massive education investment in the poorest provinces of southern Mindanao. Sure textbooks and classroom acquisition can be corrupted, but 80% of education investment is teacher salary. In a nation where one teacher rotates between two classrooms of sixty children, more and better teachers seems a logical entry point for foreign assistance.

Afghanistan – towards inclusion

17 February 2016, *Online Opinion*

As most of us return to work, at least 1,500 Australians serving in the Middle East did not have the luxury of seeing their families this holiday season.

Afghanistan is the world's poorest nation outside Africa. Now, after a decade of western deployment and eight billion Australian dollars, it's no longer the most dysfunctional. Since 2004, Australia has been a foundation partner in what is now an international coalition of forty-five nations. Despite that, 85% of the $5.7 billion reconstruction price tag is borne by the US, with Australia's development aid contribution coming in at fourth.

Back in 1992, I worked in Kabul's Red Cross hospital and later with a landmine clearing team in the north. Even then, it was believed that Afghanistan was the place where good money followed bad and where colonial aggressors were bled dry then spat out. Grinding out the precursors to a more civil Afghanistan appears to be a waiting game with a missing participant; the local population.

For the first time, there is now an admission that our presence in Afghanistan is predicated on improved long-term conditions rather than any time frame. It's about facing up to the fact that we are here for at least another generation, rather than clutching at exit strategies. Afghanistan has seen cycles of hope, decay, war then stabilisation again. Arresting that cycle starts with offering a trellis of opportunity that allows Afghans to take responsibility, make mistakes and try again.

The heart of this approach is Operation *Resolute Support*. Australia has committed $80 million annually to this initiative, focused on training a more effective Afghan defence force plus another $20 million annually for domestic policing. We have also partnered with the U.K. and New Zealand to train a thousand Afghan Army officer recruits annually. This targeted investment is producing leaders, not just lieutenants.

Importantly, the recruitment of women to the Afghan National Academy is a key priority and relies on guarantees of safe accommodation, career paths, language skills and cultural respect. Last year, it was a young Afghan woman who graduated top of class.

But in a test of Coalition cohesion and Afghan capacity, troop commitments have been wound down from 150,000 back in 2012 to just 15,000 today. Now is the time for the Afghan army to step up, make the strategic calls and be nimble enough to make them quickly. Australians are deeply engaged in that process; grinding away the patronage culture that encourages corruption and or incompetence in the worst possible roles.

As we enter 2016, media reports lead most at home to assume Australia is withdrawing and Afghanistan is on the verge of collapse. However, the clear message on the ground is that, while fragile, the Afghan government is holding. The reality is that just one in ten locals support the Taliban which is active in just fifteen of 400 provinces. In August last year they delivered three bombing attacks and just four since then. Compared to intensities of the past, that is hardly a fire storm.

Now that the Coalition is knee-deep in the Middle East, we must leave on our terms, by keeping our mission is targeted, fair, and above all effective. Civil and democratic society starts with suppressing militant extremism because it provides the time for a new generation to get an education, jobs and experience modest levels of prosperity that make the alternatives less attractive. Knowing first-hand that Afghanistan hasn't seen those conditions for generations, I know they won't let this opportunity slip now.

Andrew Laming is a Coalition MP deployed in the Middle East in January 2016. He Chairs the standing committee on Education and Employment.

Uncertainty grows in Israeli-Palestinian dispute

13 February 2019

A micro-brewery in Palestine exporting local beer to a dozen nations is inspiring enough. Even more so when owner Elena Khouri describes her beloved beer's short journey to the Haifa port, which takes three days. Palestinian product she tells me, can only be transported on half palettes for security reasons. It is last priority at Israeli checkpoints and when it misses curfew, has to sit on the roadside overnight. These frustrations mean the short road journey through Israel costs her company more than shipping it to Europe.

For the four million Palestinians in the West Bank, an economy on life-support is now the norm. Over 400 new Israeli settlements have spread like grapeshot across the Palestinian West Bank, many of them connected with Israeli-only roads. For Israel, these new communities represent 'facts on the ground;' a creeping dividend from political paralysis. A two-state solution seems less and less likely every day; replaced by a one-plus version; Israel and whatever is left.

Despite having comparable populations, Israel's $360 billion dollar economy is sixty times the size of the Palestinian authority. While security has improved for both sides, the economic dividends are tragically asymmetric.

Palestinians lay fault exclusively at the feet of Israel. Top of their list include harassment at checkpoints, settlement creep, water insecurity and alleged seizure of farmland. Israel even collects tax revenue from Palestinian areas; returning it less a 3% service fee.

But separating Israel's antipathy from the broader psychological malaise of occupation is not easy. But one thing is clear. Palestinian leverage is waning. They can withdraw recognition of Israel, end security cooperation or ramp up international pressure; none of which has showed much bite. Less than a quarter of Israeli territory is still on the negotiation table. Add to that the Trump administration snuffing out much of their aid flow and the US Embassy relocation to Jerusalem and you can see why there is a sense of despondency.

There is also pessimism about how Jerusalem can be a bisected capital. Palestinian East Jerusalem continues to fill with Israeli settlers. That makes a simple east/west partition of the city more complex. Each day that passes, it seems options for Palestinians narrow.

One approach is to uncouple the fate of West Bank from dysfunctional Hamas-controlled Gaza. Physically connecting these two regions into a single Palestinian state now seems improbable. Gaza is in appalling condition and the likelihood of Hamas collaborating to form a government of unity appears slim. While proponents long for a single Palestine, the reality seems brighter with the West Bank forging its own future, leaving Gaza for a later date. The current stalemate serves only Israel's interest.

To do that, Palestinians must embark unilaterally on nation-building even if done unilaterally. Statehood begins with a population registry and land book to document Palestinian private title in the zones they share or control. Thanks to better tax collection, aid has shrunk from 50% to 15% of revenues, which enhances capacity building and self-determination. That must also include a transition of UN-run refugee health and education services back to local control.

But economic development is far from fine-tuned, with youth unemployment exceeding 70% in Gaza and limited prospects for school leavers. Beyond the lucky few gaining entrance to university, the remainder fend for themselves in a highly informal vocational and trades sector.

Economic opportunity is critical because optimism for the peace process has long since evaporated. Mistrust and corruption concerns ran above 90% of respondents in a recent survey of the Palestinian population. At these levels, a return to conflict or extremism can't be excluded.

Hamas has dealt themselves out of the picture. Despite renouncing violence last year, it isn't always that way on the ground. Those in the West Bank quip that Hamas is yet to learn that non-violence is more than turning up peacefully; it is about protesting and re-turning home peacefully as well.

At every turn, the next step to peace is blocked by intractable stances on so-called final-status issues. This creates a stalemate where parties have either subconsciously or deliberately poisoned the next chess move with inflexible positions.

The other hurdle for Palestinians is their central role in encourag-ing the boycott and divestment of Israeli goods. Little wonder Israel has little time for exporters like Elena. Ironically the West Bank is peppered with UN-run access coordination units, but they monitor aid flows and ignore trade flows altogether.

After half a century of calling Israel to account for their actions, Palestinian leaders remain in a state of immediacy; proud that they have never acquiesced but with few wins to show for it. Akin to Ni-etzsche's reflexive subject, UN presence perpetuates victimhood, and removes much of the requirement for the Palestinian leadership to account for their actions. In what should be negotiation between equals, Palestinian incoherence at local level allows Israel to brush off the barrage of UN resolutions as 'out of touch with reality.'

Palestinians crave freedom, but once seized, will inevitably be bound again by economic reality. By legitimising themselves with the fight for freedom, their populations are in a suspended state of suffering with the promise that their endurance will one day be duly rewarded. Delayed freedoms may be worth the struggle, but not if the dividend is shrinking before their eyes. That is why the Palestin-ian Authority needs to talk more about responsibilities, too many of which rest with the international community.

Trump doesn't have to blink, but if North Korea is any indication, he could change the game and jolt the process into gear. If he doesn't, it appears the Palestinians are happy to play a waiting game to see off Netanyahu, hope Trump loses in 2020 and hold together their own leadership in the meantime.

Israel continues its push into the West Bank because it can get away with it. Its actions are expansionary, but at a pace designed to minimise legal, online or international resistance. Negotiation was started some say, only to ensure it failed, and in order to demonstrate its futility. While only a minority of Israelis are psychologically invested in the settlement push, it is less clear if they think it advances their cause or makes bloody conflict more likely. Most would take a non-violent way out if it was offered.

A shared Jerusalem with twin administrative wards and a historic quarter for free movement is hardly an impossible dream. But far more important is resolving Palestinian land ownership, water misallocation and their freedom of movement. Only these steps will allow a shift from handouts to economic development and a substantial improvement in standards of living for Palestinians in the West Bank.

12
first speech 2004

First speech to Parliament

17 November 2004

I begin with three life events that for me have been high-water marks. The first was in the highlands of Papua New Guinea as a child, where my parents made an unusual career choice. It is also an unusual place to begin this speech. My dad planned expeditions into the remote parts of that land to build a platform for independence. I stayed at home doing correspondence classes with my mum and my sisters, Susie and Julie, whose unconditional love continues to this day.

In 1992, when clearing landmines in Afghanistan, I lost my two great friends, Tim Goggs and Julian Gregson in a landmine accident in Kare Samir. In that village today, those two fine, courageous men are remembered with a small plaque written in English and in Farsi. That inscription reminds us that in peace, as well as in war, we make the ultimate sacrifice sometimes to build and preserve what Australia has never lost: free and fair elections and democracy.

Forward then to where Australia took centre stage in the reconstruction of Timor L'orosae. In rebuilding that shattered health system, I learnt that if there is one thing greater than opportunity, it is removing the barriers to opportunity for others. That country today is still a free and peaceful land.

Each of these three stories reminds me that human endeavour, however infinitely small, forever lays a platform for the acts that come after. It is no different in Bowman, because today marks the first time that the Redlands area has a dedicated seat in this parliament. There is in that place a unique identity that you can perhaps trace back to 1842, when for the first time the squatters tried to cut Brisbane out of the loop and export their produce directly through the port of Cleveland. They hoped that it would one day become the capital of Queensland. Obviously, as history records it, Governor George Gipps sailed into Moreton Bay and unfortunately his arrival was at low tide. As he stepped out of the boat and into thigh-deep mud – or "deep nastiness" as it was recorded – the fate of Cleveland was sealed. Brisbane gained the honour of being the capital of Queensland, as well as the status of being the main port.

But that bitter disappointment is tempered somewhat after 160 years. We now know we have a fantastic, unique identity and a wonderful bayside foreshore. As you drive from Brisbane over those somewhat soporific undulations of Bonner—my apologies to the new member, but congratulations on your election—and you arrive at the bayside where that bay breeze greets you, you know you are in a very special community. We still have memories of the pioneer families, such as the Sherrins, the Benfers, the Biggs and the Balfours. Before them are the Quandamooka and Noonuccal, whose people there recall a different time. As Oodgeroo Noonuccal almost laments to her ancestors:

> What if you came back now
> To our new world, the city roaring
> There on the old peaceful camping place
> Of your red fires along the quiet water,
> How you would wonder
> At towering stone gunyas high in air
> Immense, incredible;
> Planes in the sky over, swarms of cars
> Like things frantic in flight.

I have said that to represent Bowman is in some ways to represent Australia. No one here could feel out of place there – be they small business workers, an aspirational young family or retirees. There is a very strong environmental culture, a social sector and strong philanthropy. In the main street, you might well meet our mayor, Don Seccombe, a 1964 state cricketer, or perhaps local councillors of the calibre of Alan Beard from Alexandra Hills or Peter Dowling from Victoria Point. Or you might meet local identities: Bill Benson, Merv Genrich, Paul Satler, Al Benfer, Leo Hielscher, the Richards brothers, Alan Lucas, Sheldon College's Lyn Bishop, Norm and Alison Dean or Ernie Harrison from the Over 50s Leisure Centre.

Bowman's place in south-east Queensland is not dissimilar to Australia's position in South-East Asia. We remain a relatively untouched bayside foreshore with a touch of tradition or, dare I say, parochialism. Obviously, we are surrounded by that 200-kilometre city that stretches from Noosa all the way to the Tweed, but which somehow swerves around Redlands. Those very natural endowments now attract many people to this area. We are the No. 1 location for migration from within Queensland, although we are that little bit less well known to southern states. Once we too were the salad bowl for south-east Queensland, although now we have diversified to industry and to services. Farms have given way to families, the old drive-ins to drive-throughs and the old timber industry now to tourism. There are no highways running through Bowman to remind you of people in a rush to get to other places, nor are there stadiums, universities or grand esplanades.

In the last 55 years, Bowman is one of those few seats that has been as many years in the hands of Labor as in the hands of the Coalition, and that for me is very humbling. I also remember that for 18½ of the last 21 years, it has been in the hands of the Labor Party. For that I must acknowledge, in large part, Con Sciacca, a fine man, well regarded on both sides of this House and in my electorate. I wish him well in his future.

A generation in opposition hands explains in some way the grit and determination of many loyal Bowman workers, including Wynnum's Gordon Voltz, Audrey and John Dickey, 'General' Bob Harper, Shane Goodwin, Courtney Dore, Norma Curtis, Scott and Terri Lewis—Scott, you still have a wonderful sidestep at the age of 40, particularly when there is door-knocking to be done—Lorna Hourigan, Michael Davenport and Mat Tapsall. It is on behalf of those I have named that I thank everyone in Bowman—from the shopping centres to the community centres—for the faith that they have put in us. Thank you also to the ministers who visited Bowman: Kay Patterson, my former boss, and Ministers Abbott, Hockey, Nelson, Macfarlane and Vanstone. I also thank Christopher Pyne—who came twice.

I should also acknowledge the exemplary performance of the Queensland Liberals in the last election. It was absolutely superb. I congratulate President Michael Caltobiano, Geoffrey Greene and every elected member in both houses, from as far north as Senator Ian Macdonald right down to the border, and particularly Senate colleagues Brett Mason and George Brandis, with whom I attended university 21 years ago.

I have moved from the public service of medicine to that of politics because I love working with populations as much as with patients. This parliament offers the opportunity to turn great Australian ideas into reality; to temper the will of the powerful; to bring together disparate ideas, without ever discounting tomorrow. My story is no better told than by acknowledging those people who may never become politicians but whose work I will continue in this chamber: Fred Hollows and Frank Flynn, fathers of Indigenous health, whose ideas came to us a generation early for white Australia but a century late for Indigenous Australia—a constant reminder that, never having lived it, we can never claim to know better; Bessie Dixon, senior Lajamanu Aboriginal health worker, for whom the health of her Walpiri people has been a lifetime cause; Professors Hugh Taylor, Bart Currie and John Mathews, who mix scientific discipline and public health with compassion, and who introduced me to a world of remote teachers, nurses and researchers in Indigenous Australia; Chris Rogers, Frank Martin and Ralph Higgins—three exceptional eye surgeons who made room for an odd-fitting aspirant; and my two great teachers, Abram Chayes from the Harvard Law School and Vittorio Falsina – an ordained Xaverian priest from Brescia in Italy – from the Harvard Divinity School, who both, tragically, taught me in their final year of life. Your intellectual energy reoriented my views on international conflict, development and social ethics.

I acknowledge the other family that one has in a mobile career when you are not near your own: Mavis Burke, my babysitter in Hobart; Ruth and the late Mo Hansen at Churchie; Jack and Sweetpea Hutchinson; David and Sophie Holford in Goondiwindi; Bob and Gay Macdonald in Gundagai; and Greg and Christine Neave in Darwin.

I am very proud to be a Liberal. Some may not be aware that my grandfather Charles ran for the Victorian state seat of Oakleigh in 1950. My father, Bruce, who is here today, was Queensland's member for Mooloolah throughout the 1990s and Deputy Speaker in the Queensland parliament. My parents, Bruce and Estelle, are absolutely devoted to the cause of Liberalism in Queensland – and they have to accept some responsibility for the result in Bowman.

I believe there are few better role models in public life than fellow medico Brendan Nelson, who has made an undertaking in public life to always focus on policy and never attack the person or their private life.

I am a Liberal because I share with many my own age the language of my generation: of downsizing, redundancies, bankruptcies and lay-offs in the early nineties. Clearly, these are very good times today – and I am glad that the notion that this government is merely occupying the crease on a batter's paradise is slowly being unravelled both in the general community and by the OECD in their reports. As a Liberal with an eye on social sector policy, I will also work to remove that sense that there is only one side of politics which truly cares about the needy, the sick and the vulnerable – that perhaps only one side of politics truly has the social sector at heart. I passionately believe that our schools, as well as our universities and our health system, are best served by a private-public blended model that allows people choice. That model offers internal contestation, vibrancy, accountability and responsiveness. When it is all said and done, only one side of politics has really fought for and put itself on the line for that model – and for that I stand here today.

My Bowman priorities are a fairly simple interlocking cycle of eight objectives. I guess many wonder whether a person is going to say something that is slightly controversial in their first speech. My answer is that I hope that some of the things that I am proposing do one day become regarded as fairly normal. My first objective is to have a unified approach in our schools – in starting ages, curriculum, testing, accountability and ultimately even tertiary entrance. We must have the finest university sector, both in academic and technical graduates, because ultimately, we will be judged on the world stage.

our standard of living will be determined by the sort of graduates we produce and the skills that we embed within them.

For families to be able to make long-term decisions, there must be a low interest rate environment where there is some certainty and security for the future. I cannot believe that, as recently as 10 years ago, 1,000 Bowman teenagers left high school for the dole queue – rather than for jobs as they do today. My commitment is to them. With certainty comes a willingness to enter into new enterprises, to start new businesses and to plan for the future. I would also love to work towards a simplified tax system that further cuts out the black market, the loopholes and the overly burdensome state regulation. I would like to see a tax system that allows us to continue to reduce our takings in tax as a proportion of GDP. With that sort of system, we can truly afford the health and education systems that we all aspire to.

My No. 1 health priority in Bowman will be workforce. Any first-year economist will tell you that the only way to improve bulk-billing and reduce out-of-pocket costs is to increase the number of doctors we have and to have them working in the right locations. We have a Medicare safety net, a PBS safety net and also probably the greatest piece of health policy to emerge for the last couple of decades: the private health insurance rebate, which has moved large segments of Australia off the public hospital waiting lists and has, at the same time, injected billions of dollars into the health care sector.

I would like to see more aged care places for Bowman. Sometimes the allocation formulas are not as user friendly as we would like—particularly for areas like Bowman where there is a large degree of population mobility.

Lastly, I want to engage young Australians. Our young Australians out there still do not have the faith in this parliament that I would love to see. How do I convince those young Australians that this political process is one in which they can have faith? How can I convince them that the issues that they want to talk about are ones where we can really make a difference? In Bowman, the No. 1 issue is the environment – as we boast one of those great bayside ecologies. The environment must no longer be considered as something that crowds out economic growth but rather as something that is complementary.

I am grounded by the humility of my limited knowledge. I hope I am guided, but never coloured, by my life experiences. I tell my story not to hammer some ideological stake in the ground but to celebrate the diversity of experiences that are here. Different backgrounds add to the breadth of this parliament, but where that Green Valley experience begins to colour the way you approach this place – where it colours your perceptions and becomes a way of distinguishing friend from foe – I believe that diminishes this great process.

My international experiences have been very formative. Having worked with the World Bank, the great challenge I see for the next generation will be sequencing: how we transition war-ravaged and ailing economies through the development process and to the democracy and peace that we enjoy. Where tyranny prevails, where entire economies are expropriated, where property rights, private enterprise and free elections are completely denied and where free speech and a free press are eliminated, how can we ignore the moral legitimacy to act and give these places just one shot at democracy? It has been vindicated in Timor L'orosae and in Afghanistan. I have lived in both. I have worked on the Iraqi border. I am really committed to a forward-leaning approach in international affairs and nation building.

Perhaps our great foreign policy challenge will be China, but we now have an urgent appointment with the Islamic world. With one hand, we must refuse to allow terrorism to foment trouble undisturbed in any corner of the planet; with the other hand, we must be building those economic opportunities which will, in the end, stem the flow of the disempowered who turn to fundamentalism.

I want to finish by acknowledging a couple of other people who played key roles in Bowman and also by noting that, above and beyond the last redistribution, a really great swing has been achieved in this area, with a lot of people putting their faith in us for the first time. We achieved Queensland's largest swing in 2004, and also the largest margin without the benefit of incumbency. So, I take my place in this part of the chamber, flanked by traditional coalition seats, because you were absolutely unrelenting in your expectations.

I close, as I opened, with Robert F. Kennedy:

Each time a person stands up for an ideal, or acts to improve the lot of others, or strikes

out against injustice, he sends forth a tiny ripple of hope
... these ripples build a current

that can sweep down the mightiest walls of oppression
and resistance.

While there are no mighty walls to sweep down in Bowman, there are plenty of opportunities for ripples of hope—opportunities to enrich a beloved community, to preserve our Redland character and to provide choice and opportunity for those whose faith has put me here.

also by the author

Gender Hysteria: the fall of Morrison

Truth is elusive. We obscure it with relative truths. That is the business of politics.

Control is also elusive but more sought after. It helps our relative truths prevail and it defends relative truths when threatened. Power helps confer the control we need; in general, the more control we have, the better.

Genuine truth prevails only with honesty. In its absence, truth is corroded and ultimately, so too is trust. This is a complex dynamic; where humanity prioritises those we trust over the rest. From families to workplaces to civilisations, advancement needs trust as an antecedent.

Democratic politics is Hesse's glass bead game, where our relative truths are subject to intense scrutiny. It keeps relative truths from getting out of hand. It is a mysterious and mostly qualitative world, where dark arts replace science. Outcomes are hard to predict in advance and not always for the best. But humanity is yet to design a better system.

In a civil democracy like Australia, our needs are mostly attended to. We have the luxury of apathy. Being uninterested in politics is unlikely to cost us our job, home or income. Individual enterprise addresses any remaining needs not met by the State, freeing some discretionary time to pursue our wants. When that pursuit of wants transgresses upon others, conflict and chaos is inevitable, and it must be resolved. We do that either through negotiation or with the help of the legal system. In democracies, we also have the media and politics upon which to call. These are the civilised alternatives to violence and war.

War is the last option for good reason; it is always worse than a zero-sum game. Making it the first option outside a totalitarian state requires a special set of conditions.

For those who follow public life in Australia, these are stories about those conditions. This was war by a new route, which carefully and deliberately avoided what we call normal process, or procedural fairness. There was no intention ever to lodge formal complaints, nor ever allow accusations to be independently assessed.

Two parties subverted this process for their own reasons. A Prime Minister put self-preservation above process, and with that, parts of the media unleashed. This was effectively self-promotion and profit over their own strict process, called the media code of conduct.

Every public representative has opponents willing to confect criminal accusations. Rarely however, does the media fall for it. Having a Prime Minister authenticate the accusations was exactly what they needed to unleash. When the media code is jettisoned, they move into uncharted legal waters. At this point, the media is accountable for the accusations, allowing accusers to eat popcorn and watch the entertainment.

In a civilised culture, the only way to respond is with lawyers. Soon it's a proxy war; a Japanese kabuki where the inevitable outcome is either apology, judgement or compensation. In my case, all media ultimately surrendered, though a small number were too small or insignificant to be bothered suing. My process was painful, protracted, and costly but it set about repairing a broken system and went a long way to succeeding.

Genuine #MeToo females were brave. Their harrowing journeys were rightly celebrated. With that came a bandwagon effect. Some women found solidarity in re-branding their past. Others found obliging headlines by making stuff up.

This story is also using the media, but it came in the Brittany Higgins context, which had already set a stage for brave and tearful females to make historic complaints against male perpetrators, free of being required to negotiate probing questions.

Journalists offered to 'ease them through' the process of going public, even rehearsing answers, or working on follow-up responses should the accused present any uncomfortable facts in response.

Part of the complainant journey was routinely fearing for their safety, because the accused are powerful men who will exact revenge the moment they come forward. All that was taken as gospel.

When respondents opted to defend themselves, it was framed as lacking remorse and empathy or using institutional power to unfairly silence women who deserved to be heard.

2021 was a unique political moment, generated by a confluence of media pressure on a panicked Prime Minister. Potentially seeking a scapegoat when the story dropped, he then held that position to the end of his Prime Ministership, regardless of the subsequent evidence. He was proudly unflinching to the end.

Civilised democracies have clear dispute resolution paths to make war a last resort. This is the story of what it takes to corrupt that model. This story is about how and why that happened.

www.ingramcontent.com/pod-product-compliance
Lightning Source LLC
Chambersburg PA
CBHW070338270326
41926CB00017B/3904